"The Good Ole Days"

A Celebrity Vintage Classic Coloring Book For Adults

A Sample Grayscale Coloring Page Inside

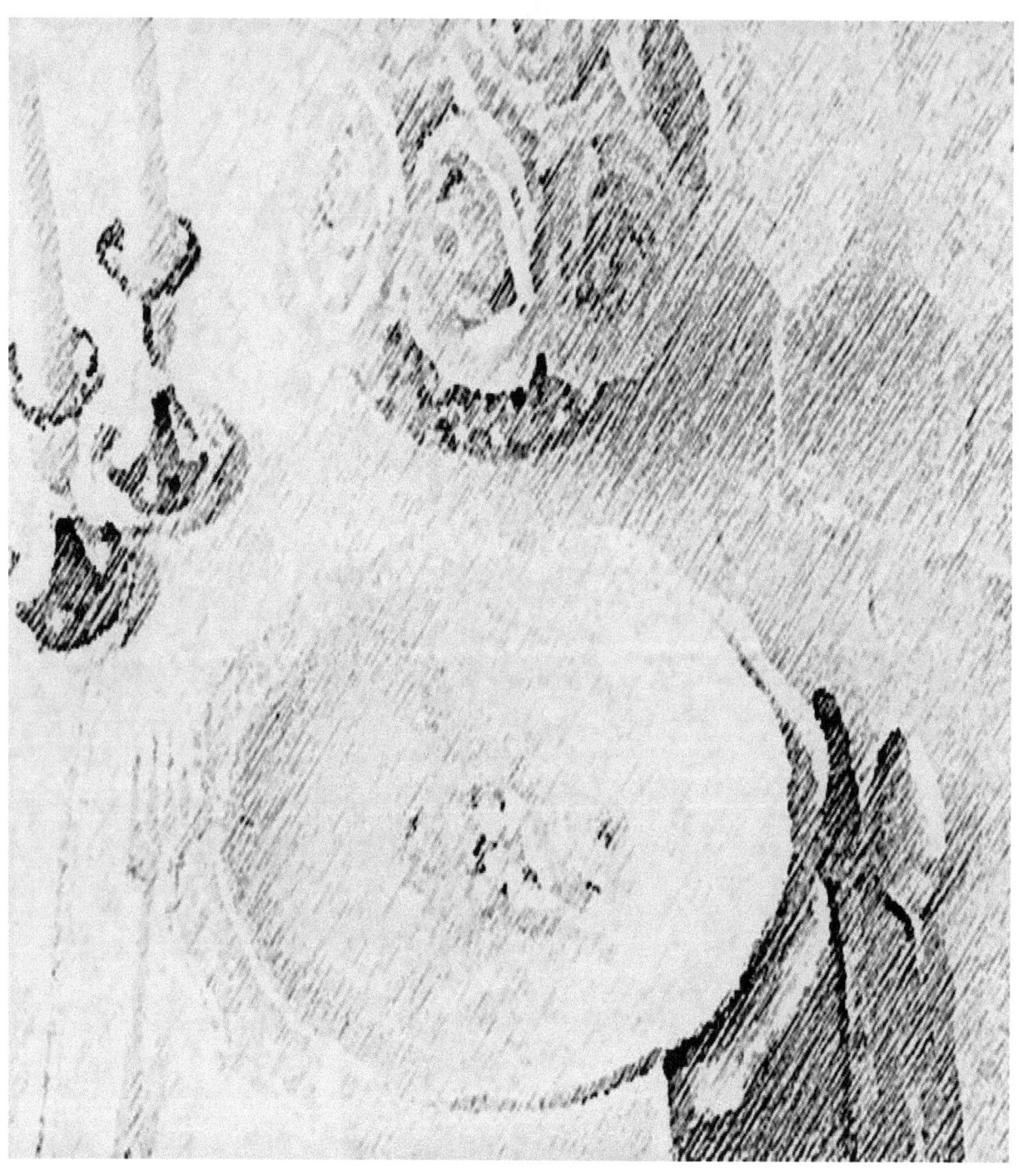

A Sample Grayscale Coloring Page Inside

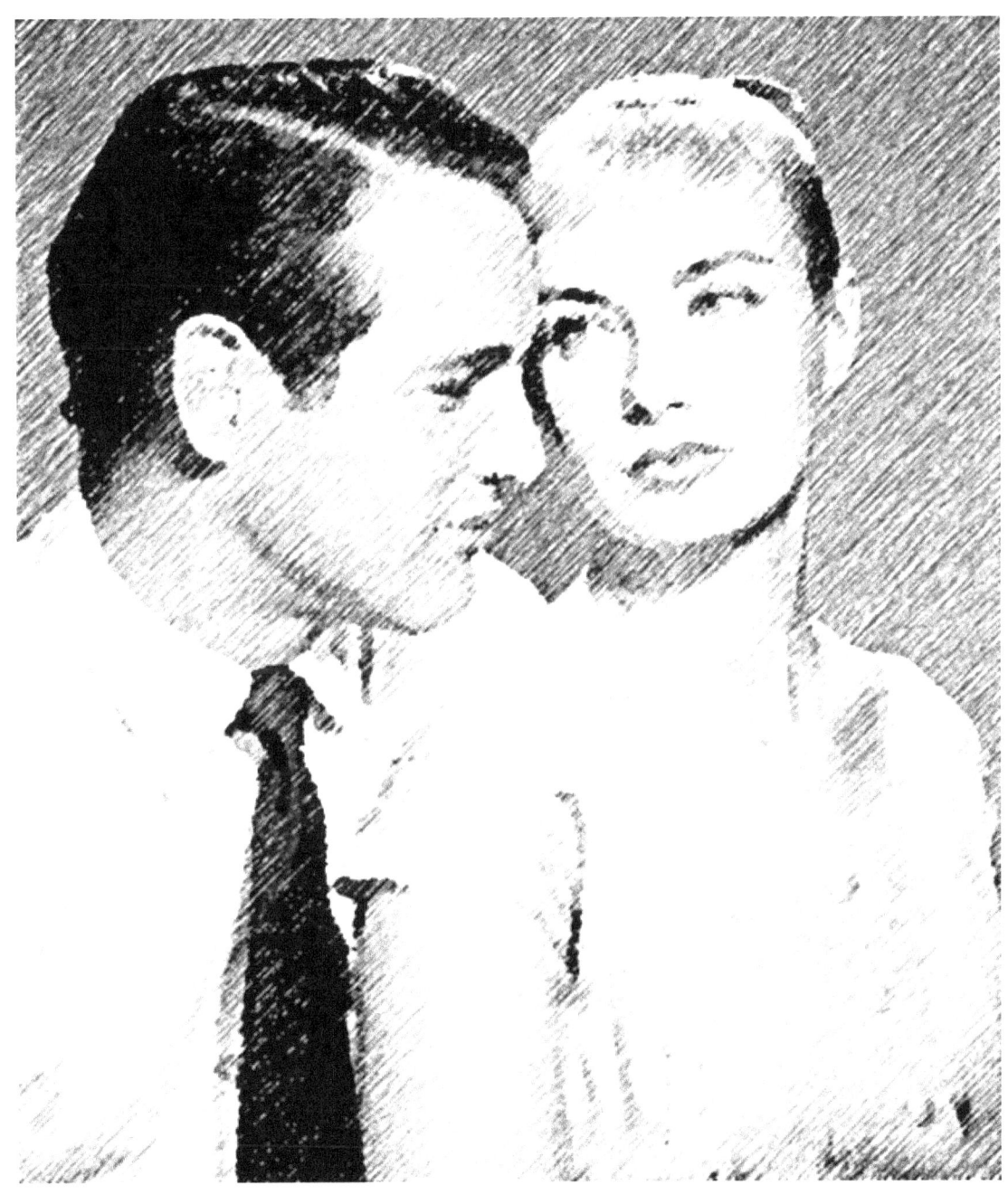

This Book Belongs To:

_____

Copyrighted Material:

All rights reserved. This publication may not be reproduced or distributed. This includes mechanical or electronic methods. Photocopying or recording is prohibited. Prior written permission must be obtained from the publisher.

Introduction:

" The Good Ole Days" Is a celebrity vintage classic. It is a coloring book intended for adults ages 65+. It contains many old-time celebrities, as well as many vintage items, from your past. It will create for you many fond memories, as it takes you back in time.

It is like paint by number, except without the numbers. You simply let your picture tell you what to do. You are guided by the shades on the page. Darkest shades get darkest colors, medium shades medium colors and white to light areas get lightest colors. Artist quality colored pencils are recommended for more intense color. Regular colored pencils are suitable, as long as they have a soft lead core. You may dip them lightly at the tip, in some petroleum jelly, for blending.

Gel pens may be used however, may not give you the three dimentional look you desire. You may blend your gel pens, by using cue tips. Never use markers or crayons on any of your grayscale coloring pages. Always place check marks and dates on all of your note taking and medication reminder pages.

This page is intended for note taking

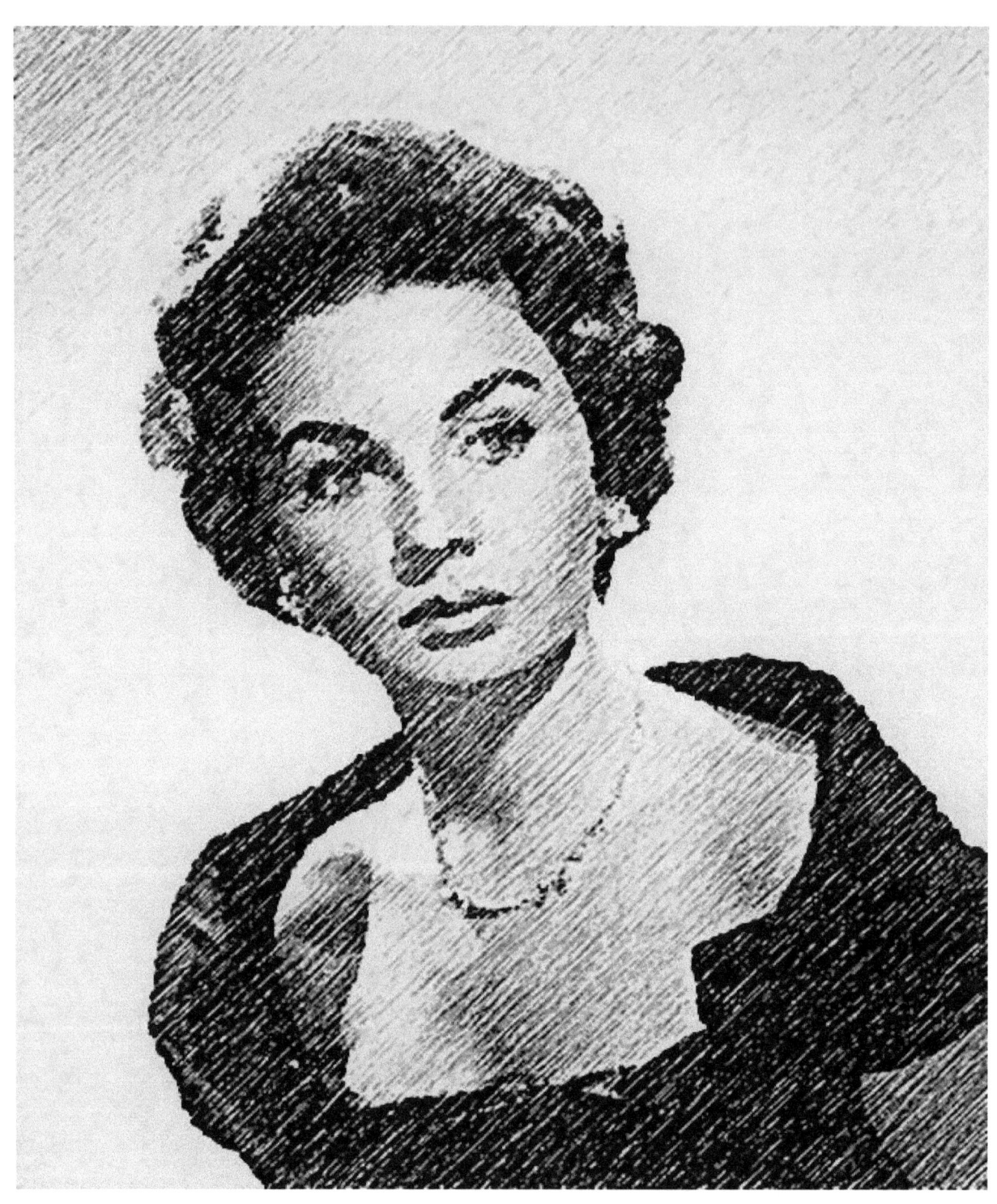

MEDICATION REMINDER

AM 1 X Daily	PM 2 X Daily	SUPPLEMENTS	NOTES

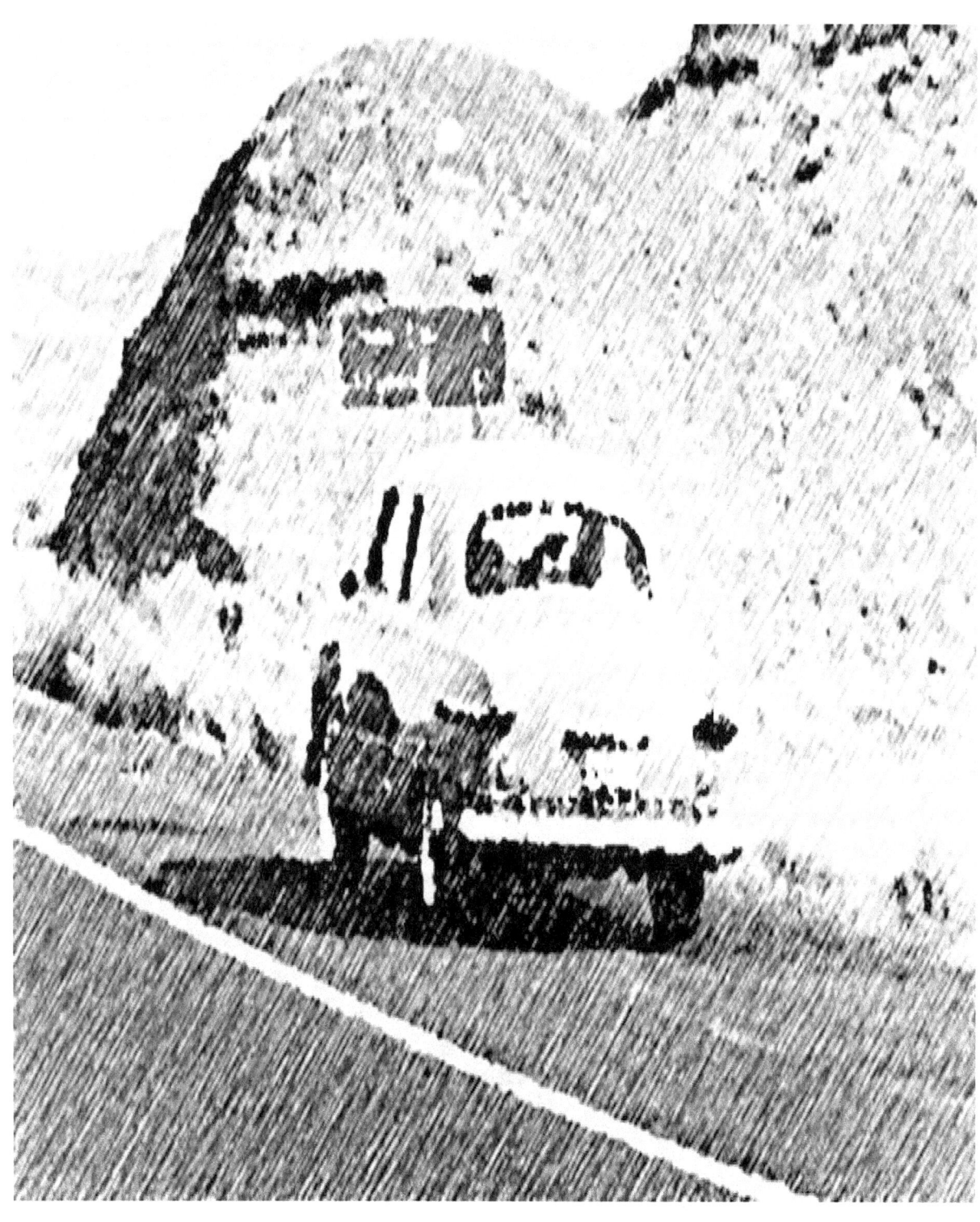

This page is intended for note taking

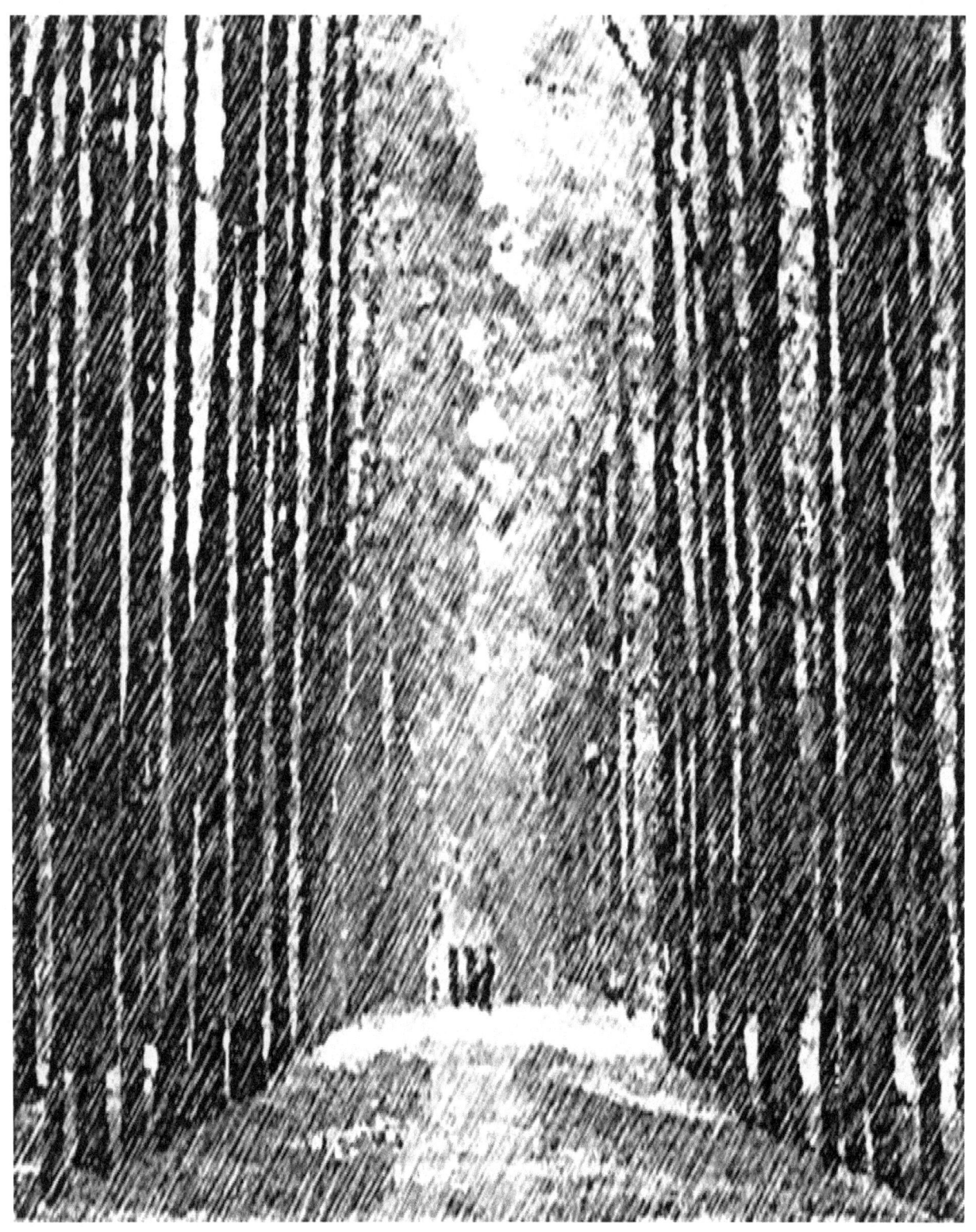

MEDICATION REMINDER

AM 1 X Daily	PM 2X Daily	SUPPLEMENTS	NOTES

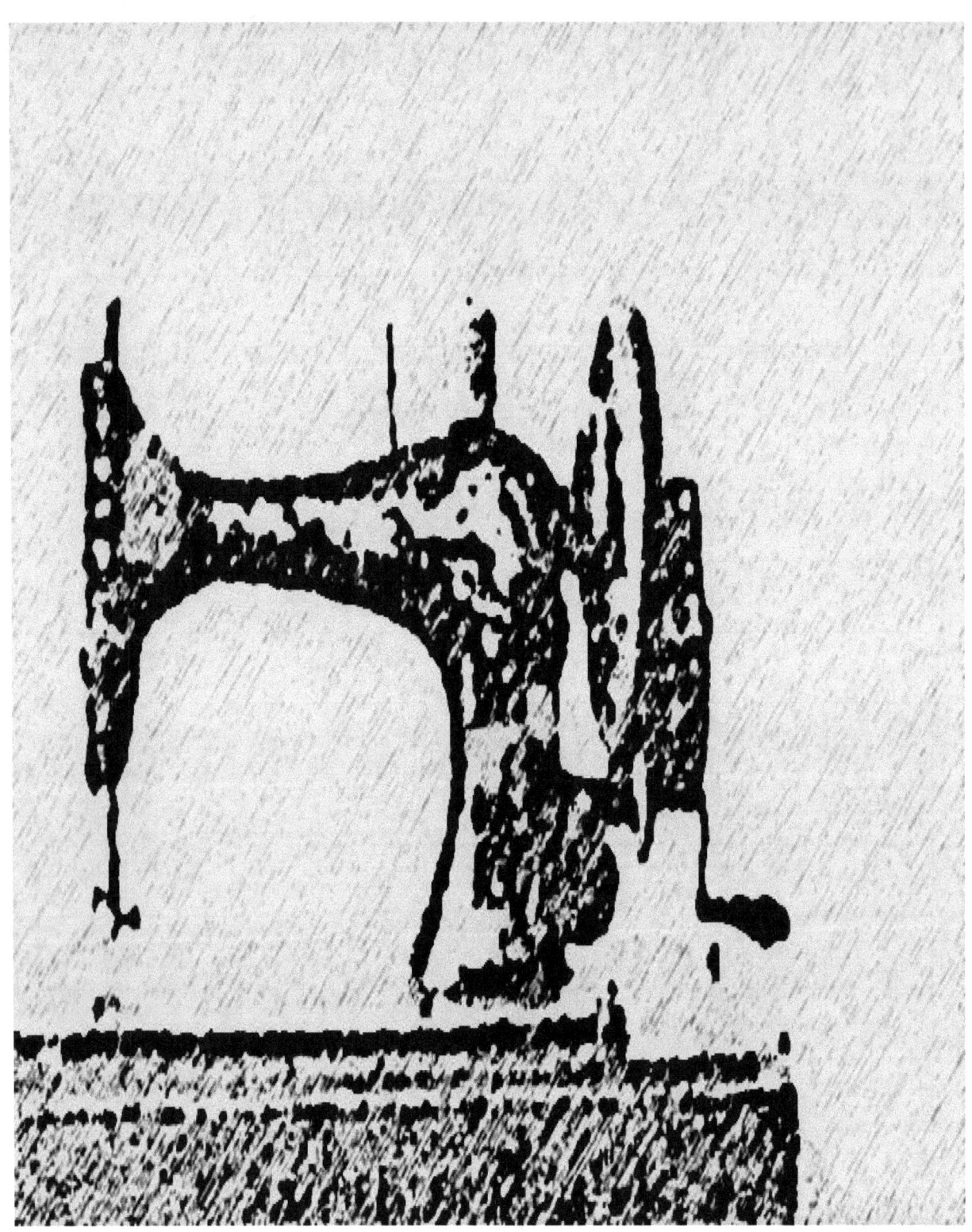

This page is intended for note taking

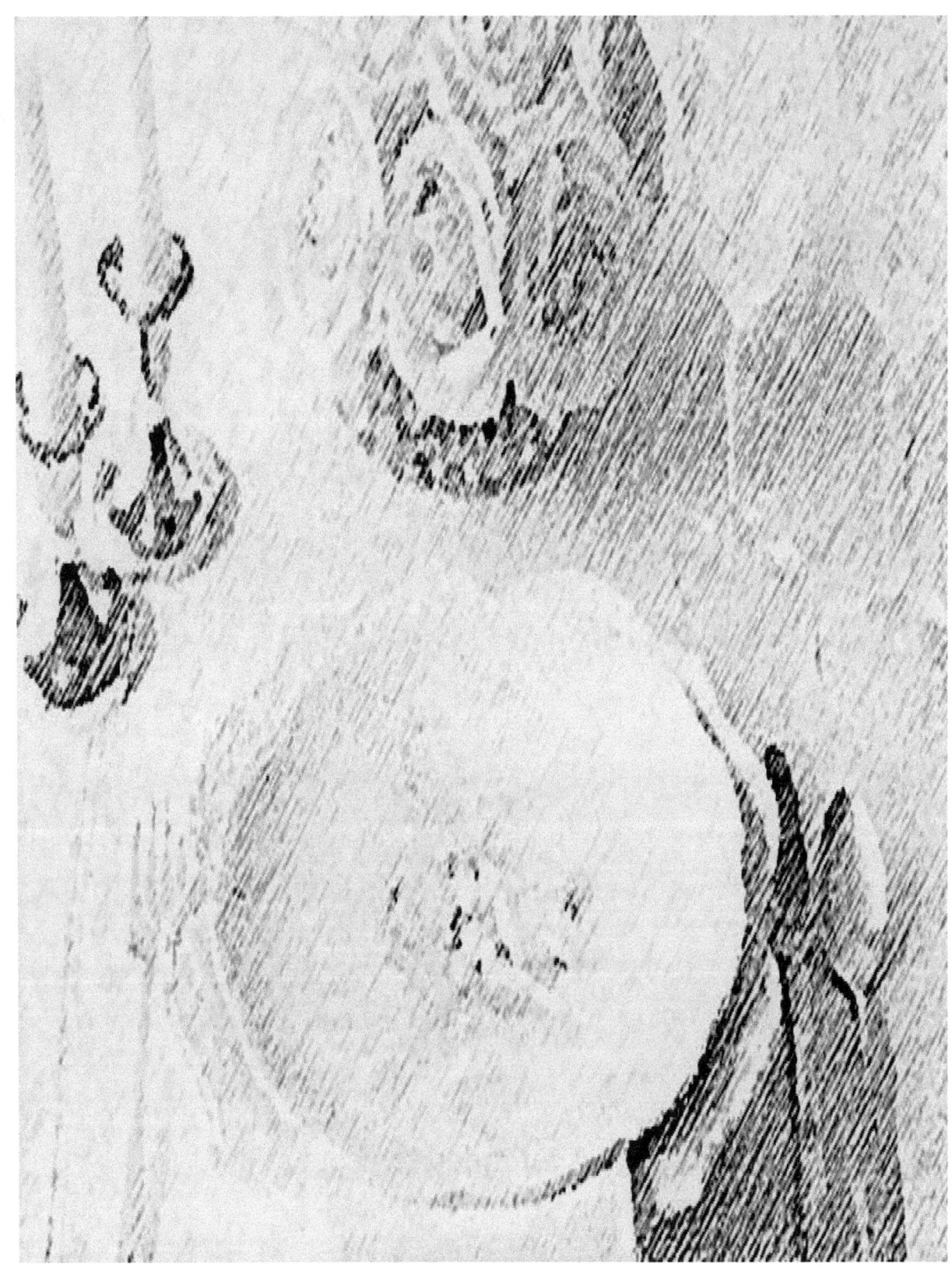

MEDICATION REMINDER

AM 1 X Daily	PM 2 X Daily	SUPPLEMENTS	NOTES

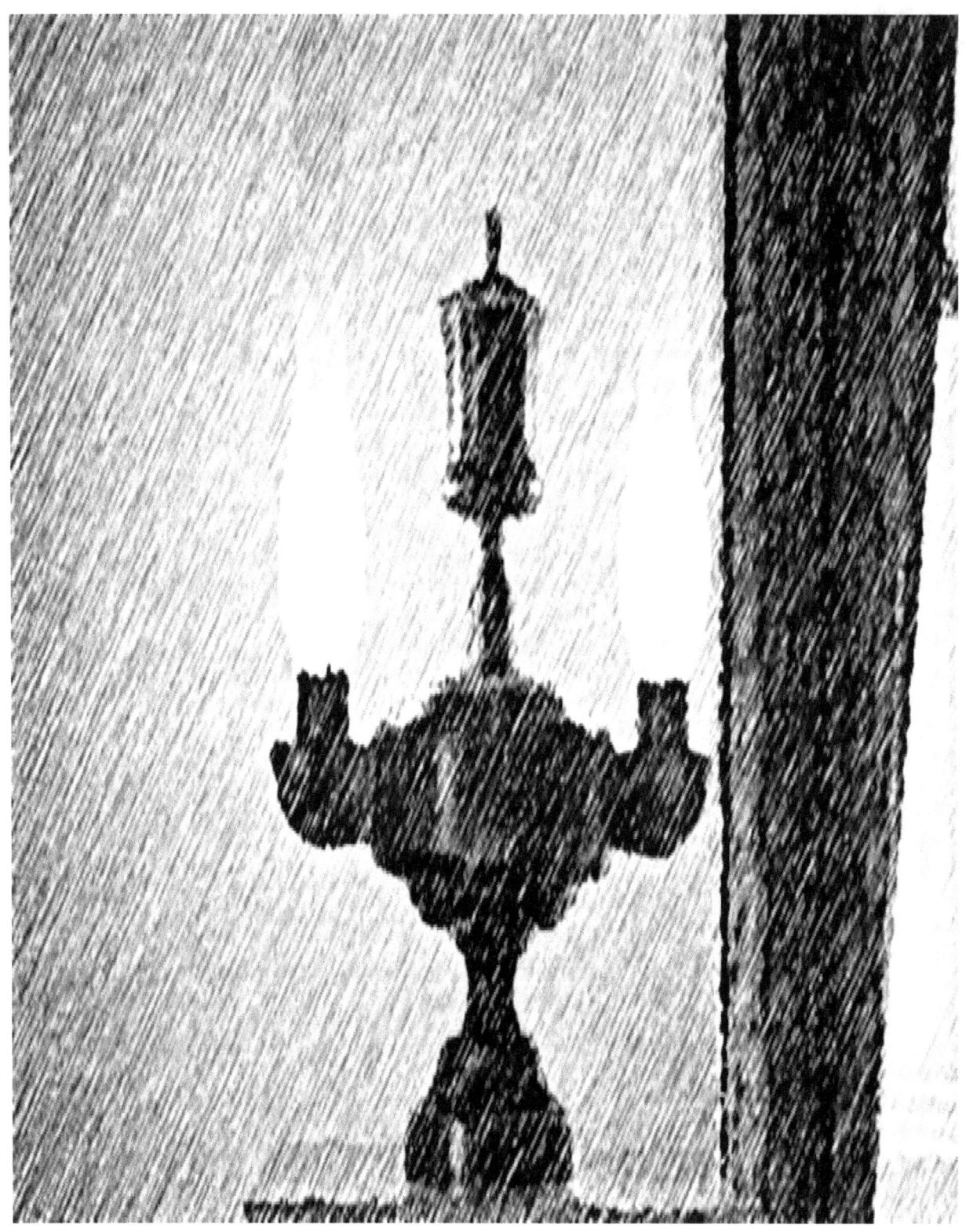

This page is intended for note taking

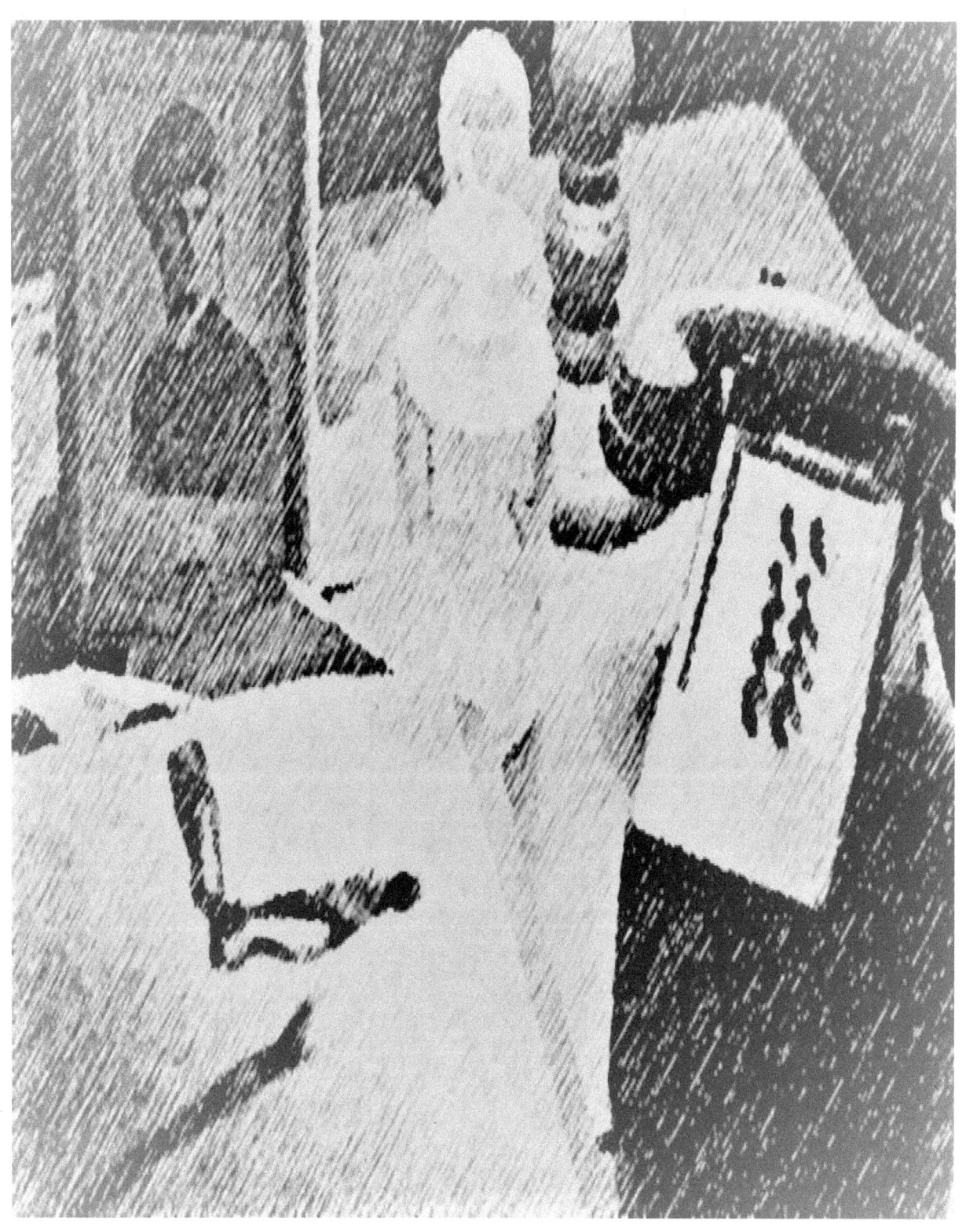

MEDICATION REMINDER

AM 1 X Daily	PM 2 X Daily	SUPPLEMENTS	NOTES

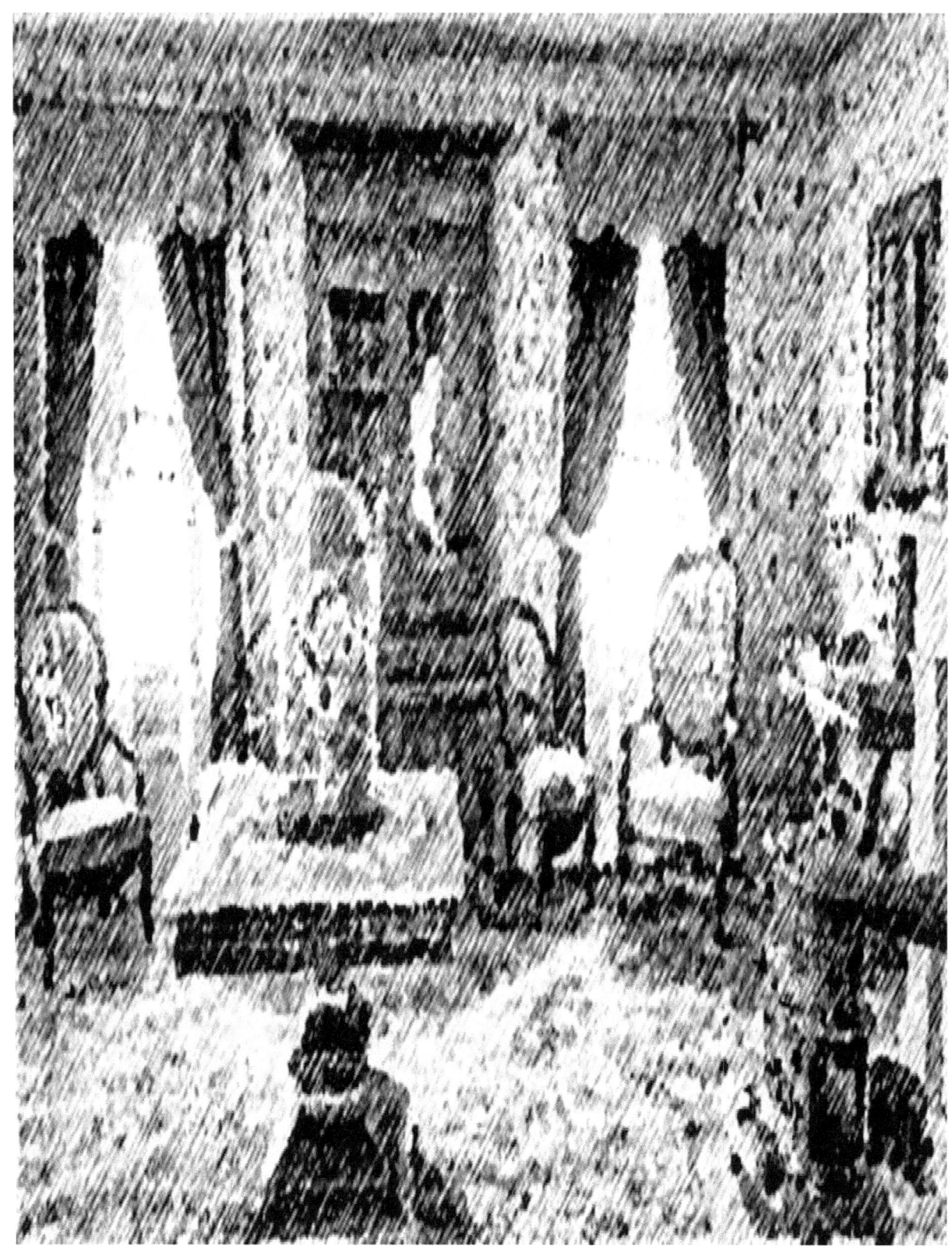

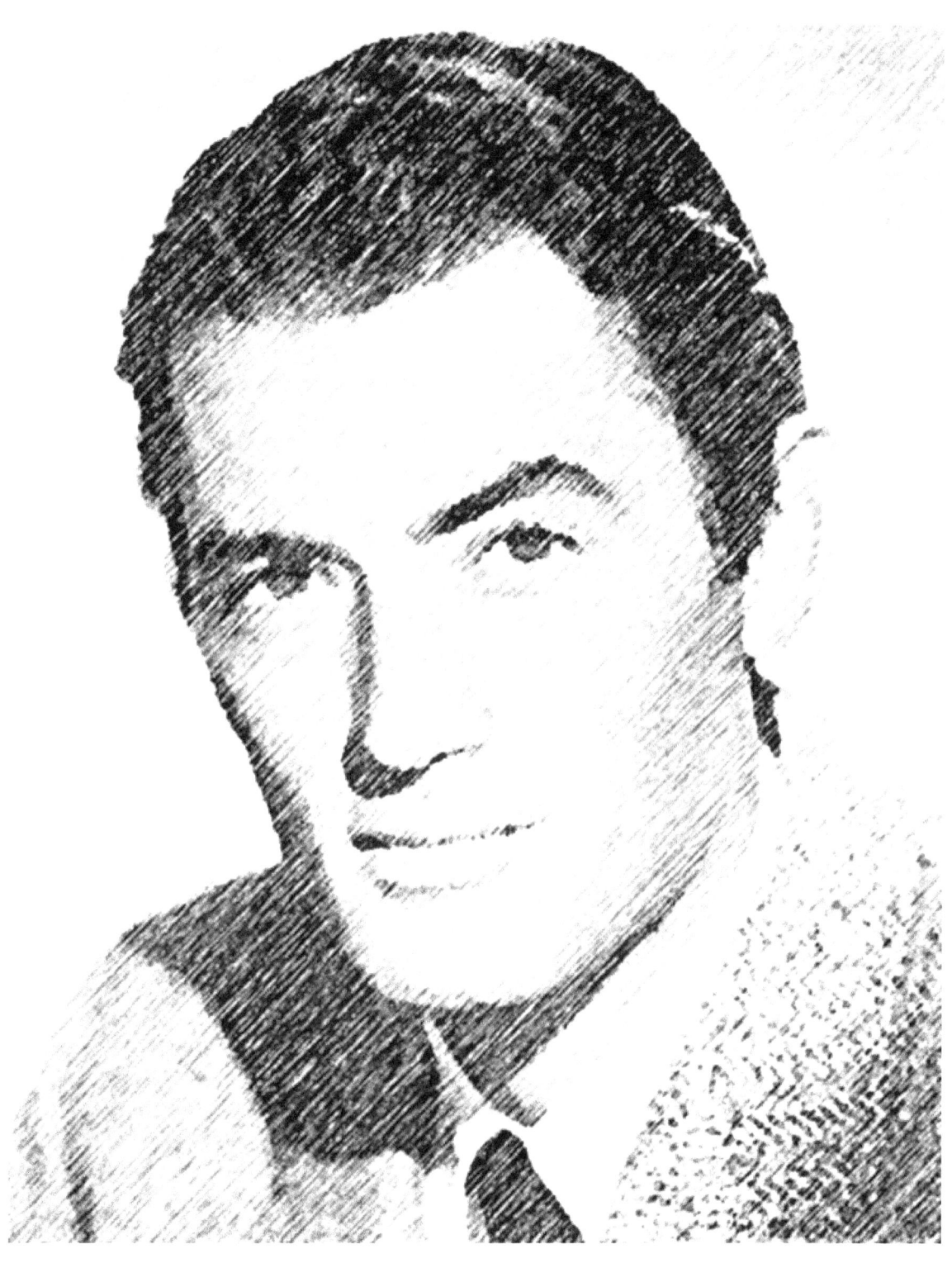

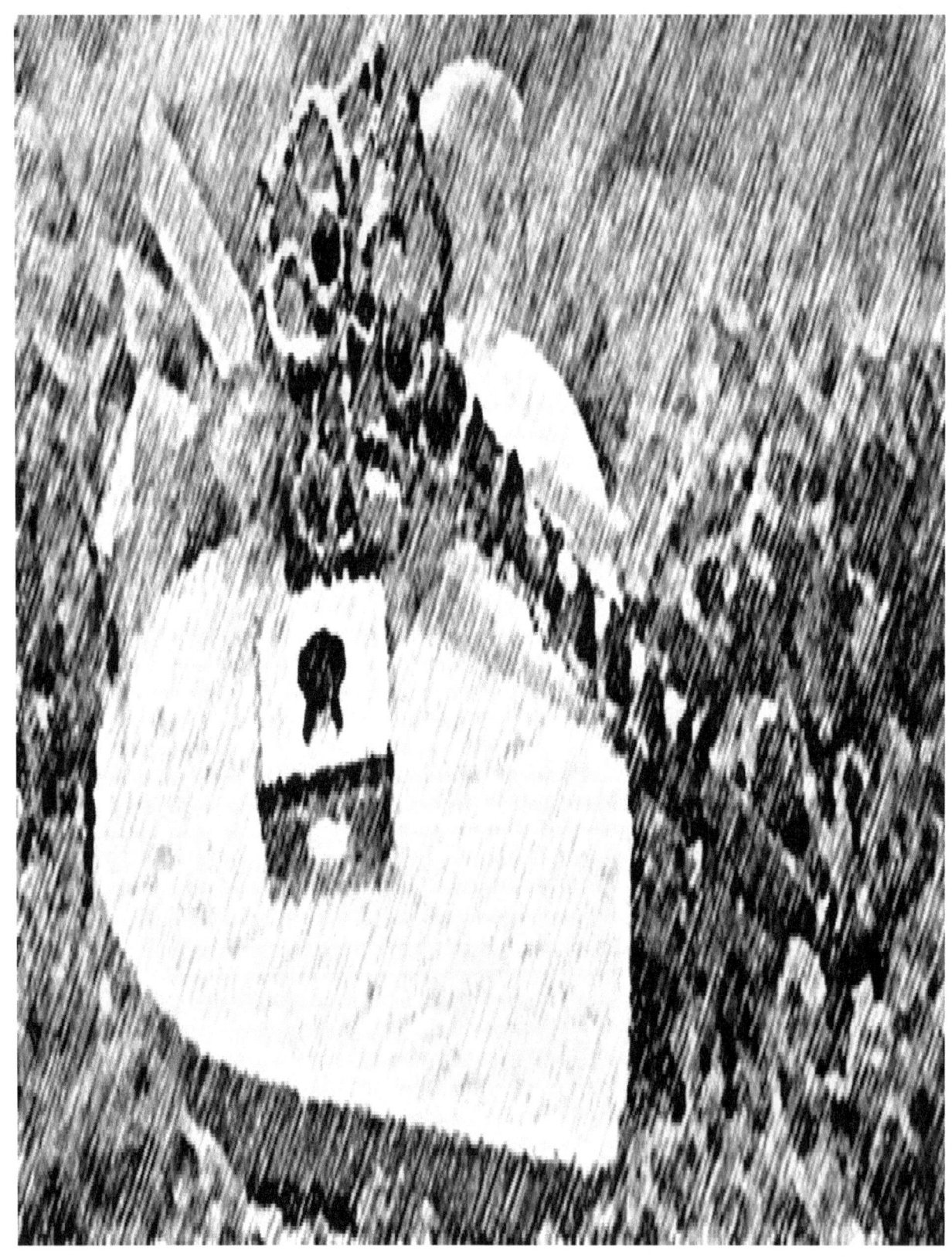

MEDICATION REMINDER

AM 1 X Daily	PM 2 X Daily	SUPPLEMENTS	NOTES

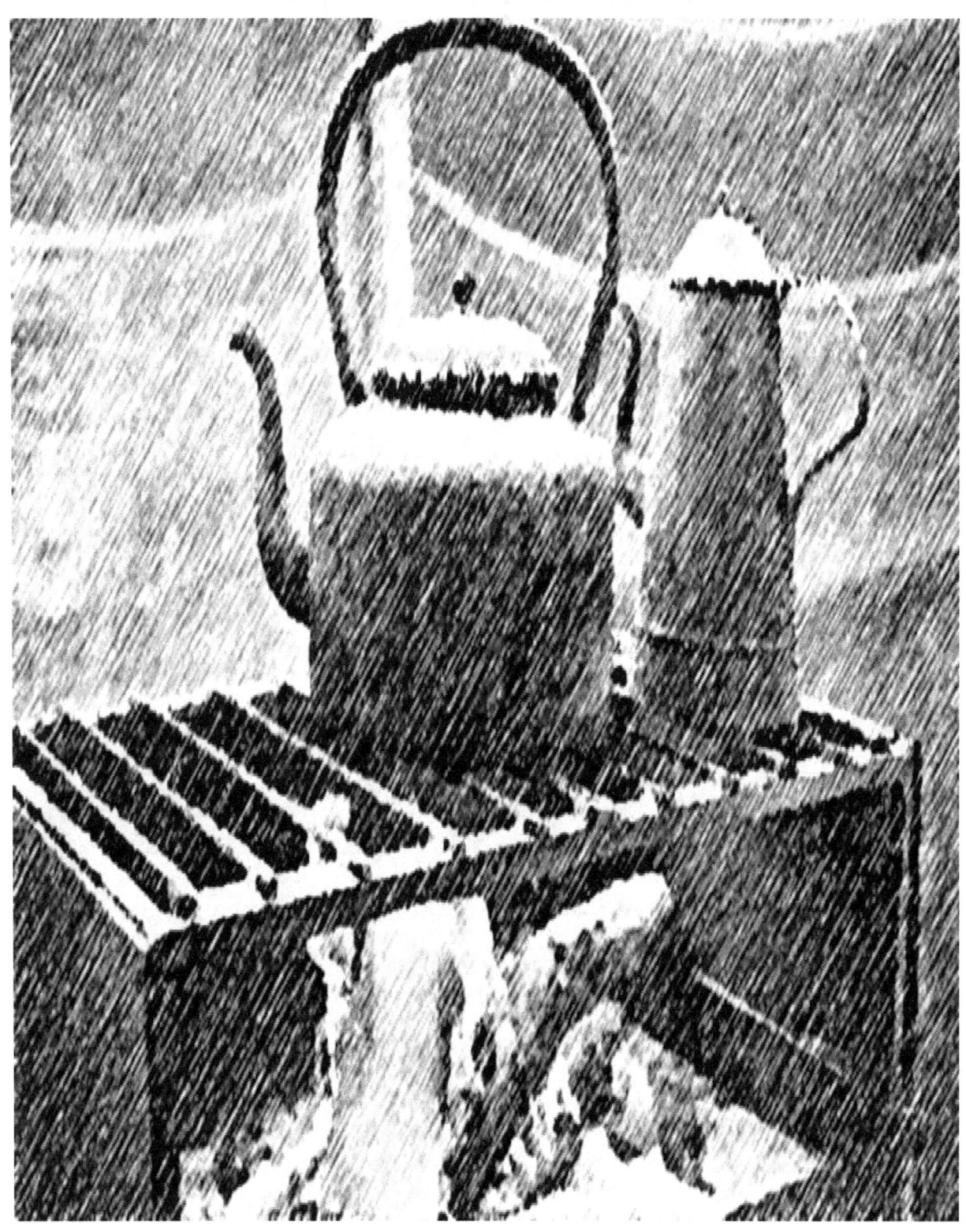

This page is intended for note taking

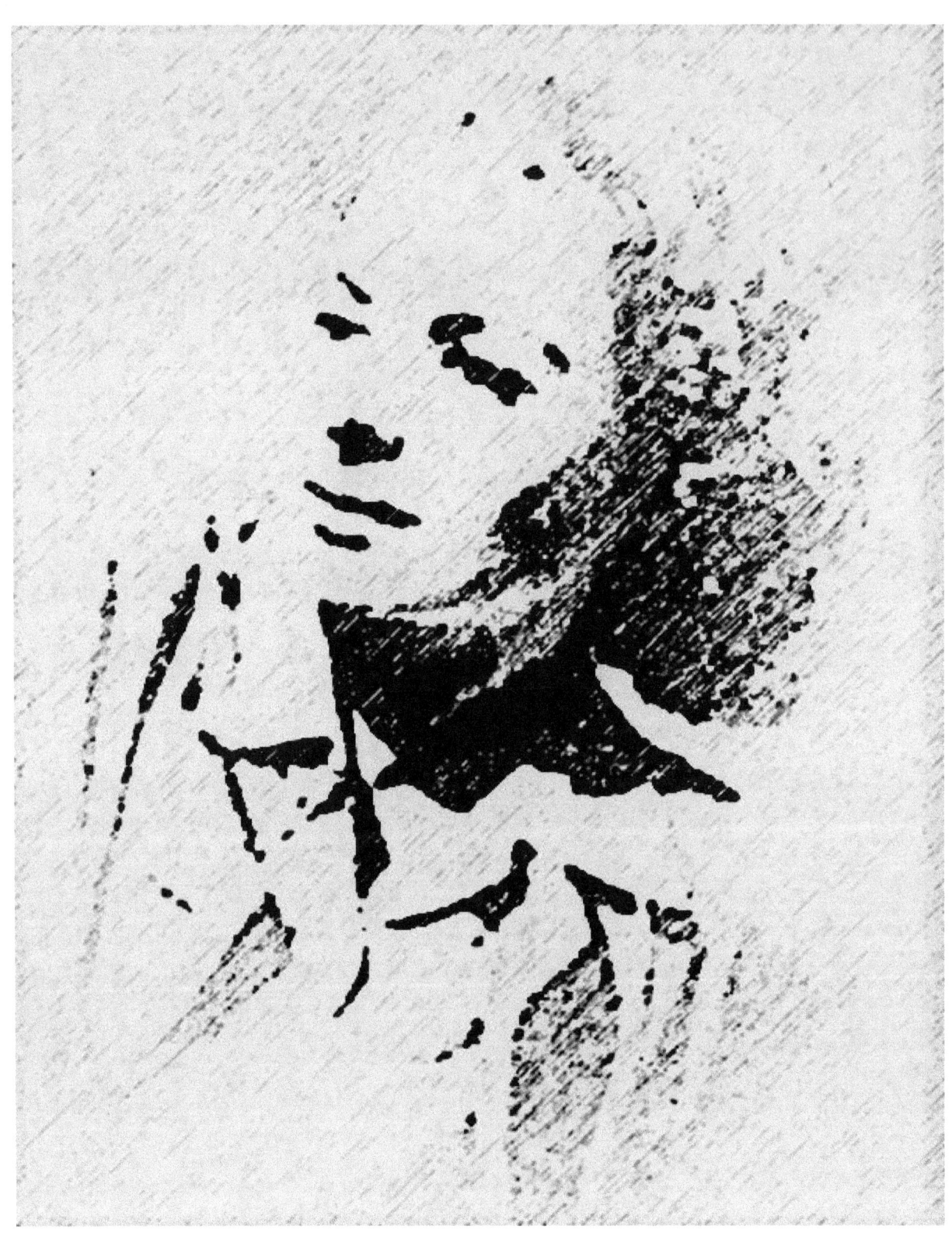

MEDICATION REMINDER

AM 1 X Daily	PM 2 X Daily	Supplements	Notes

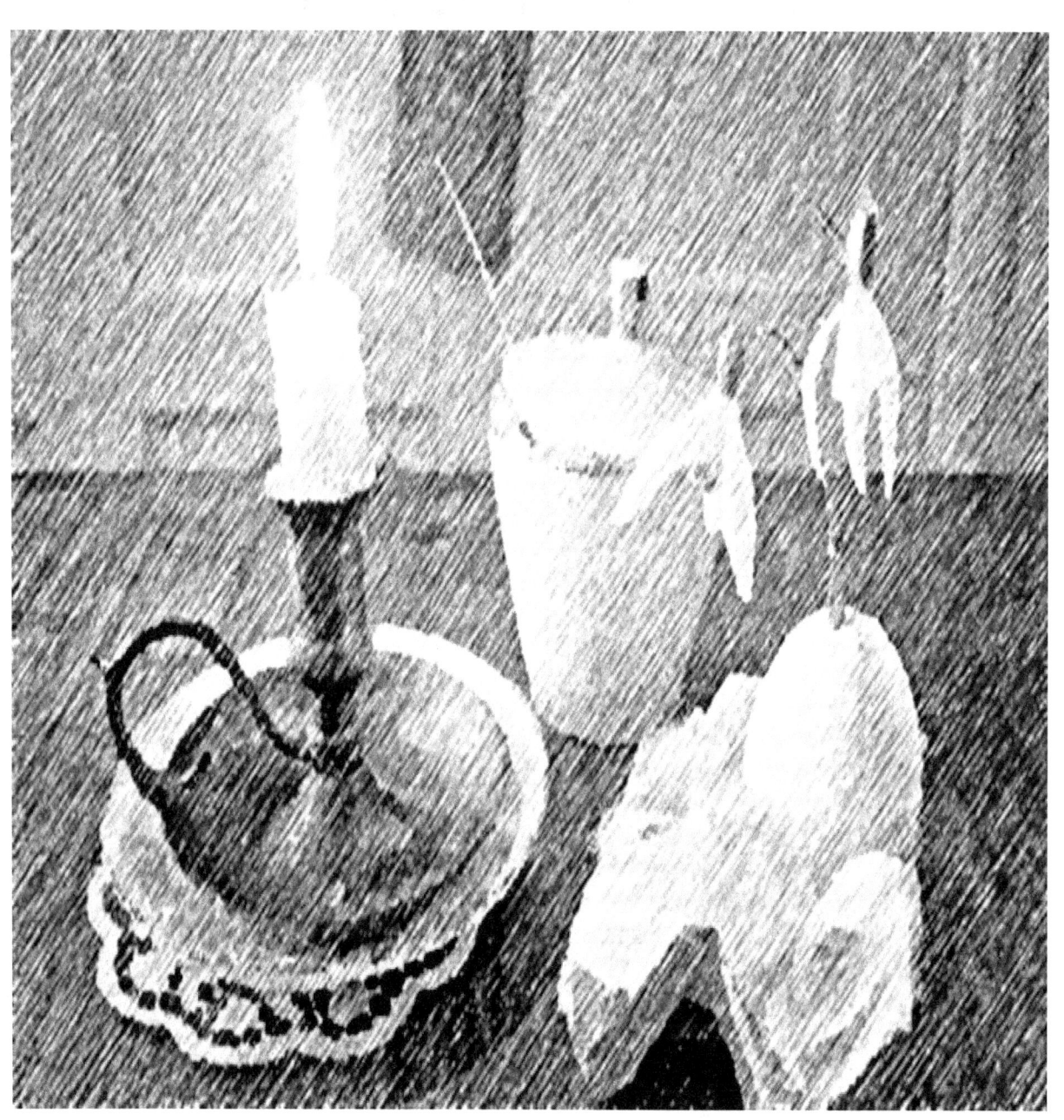

This page is intended for note taking

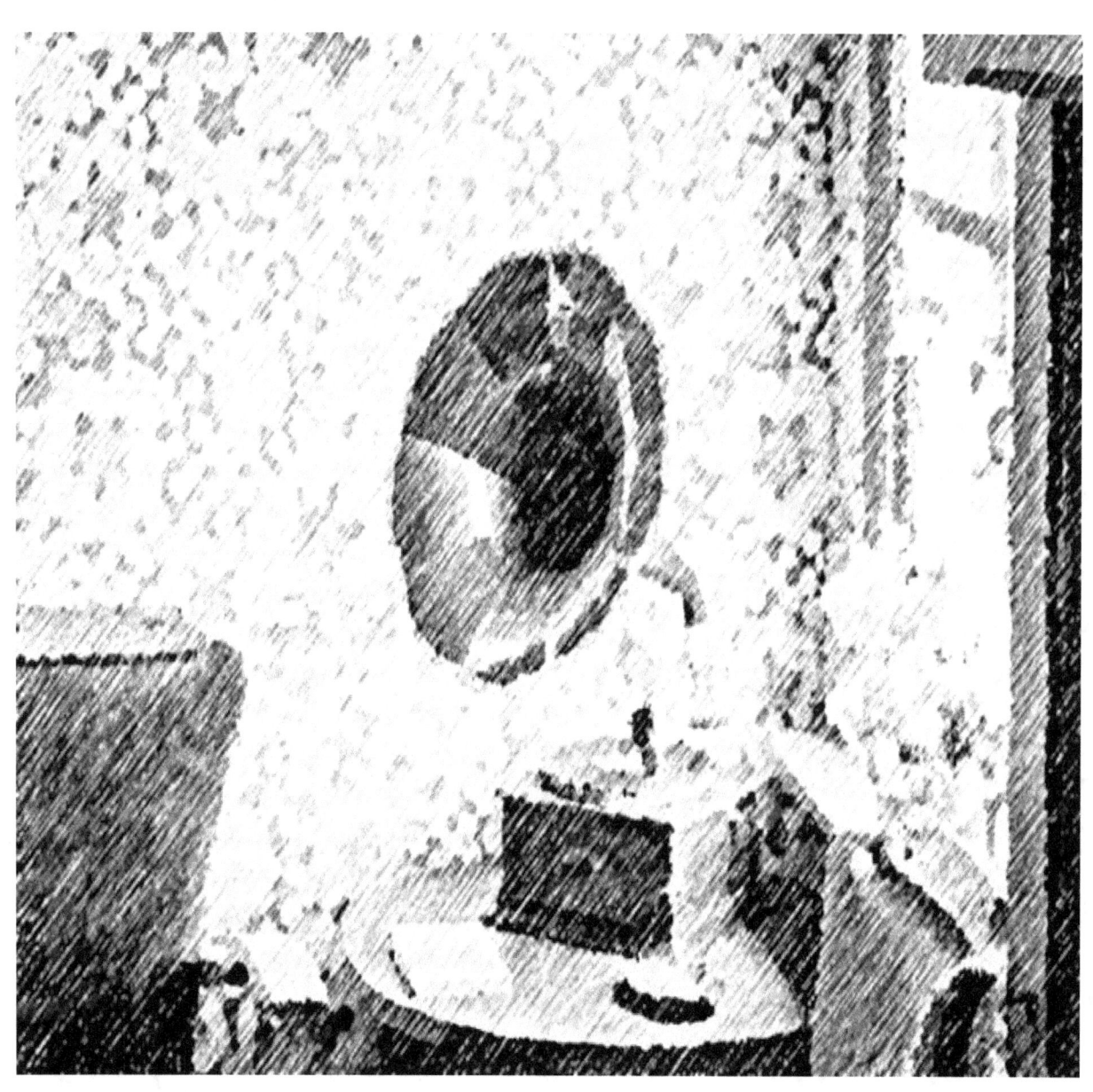

This page is intended for note taking

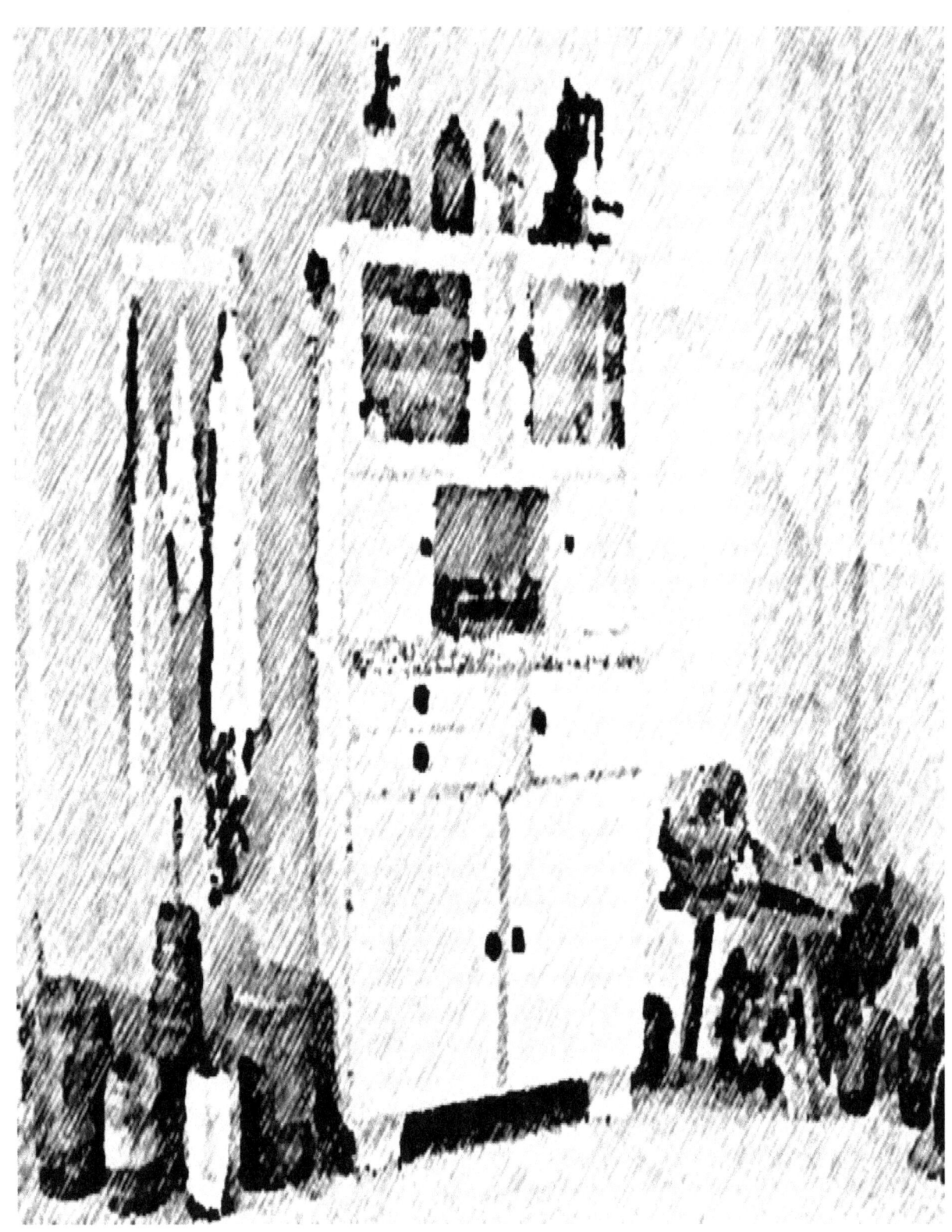

MEDICATION REMINDER

AM 1 X Daily	PM 2 X Daily	SUPPLEMENTS	NOTES

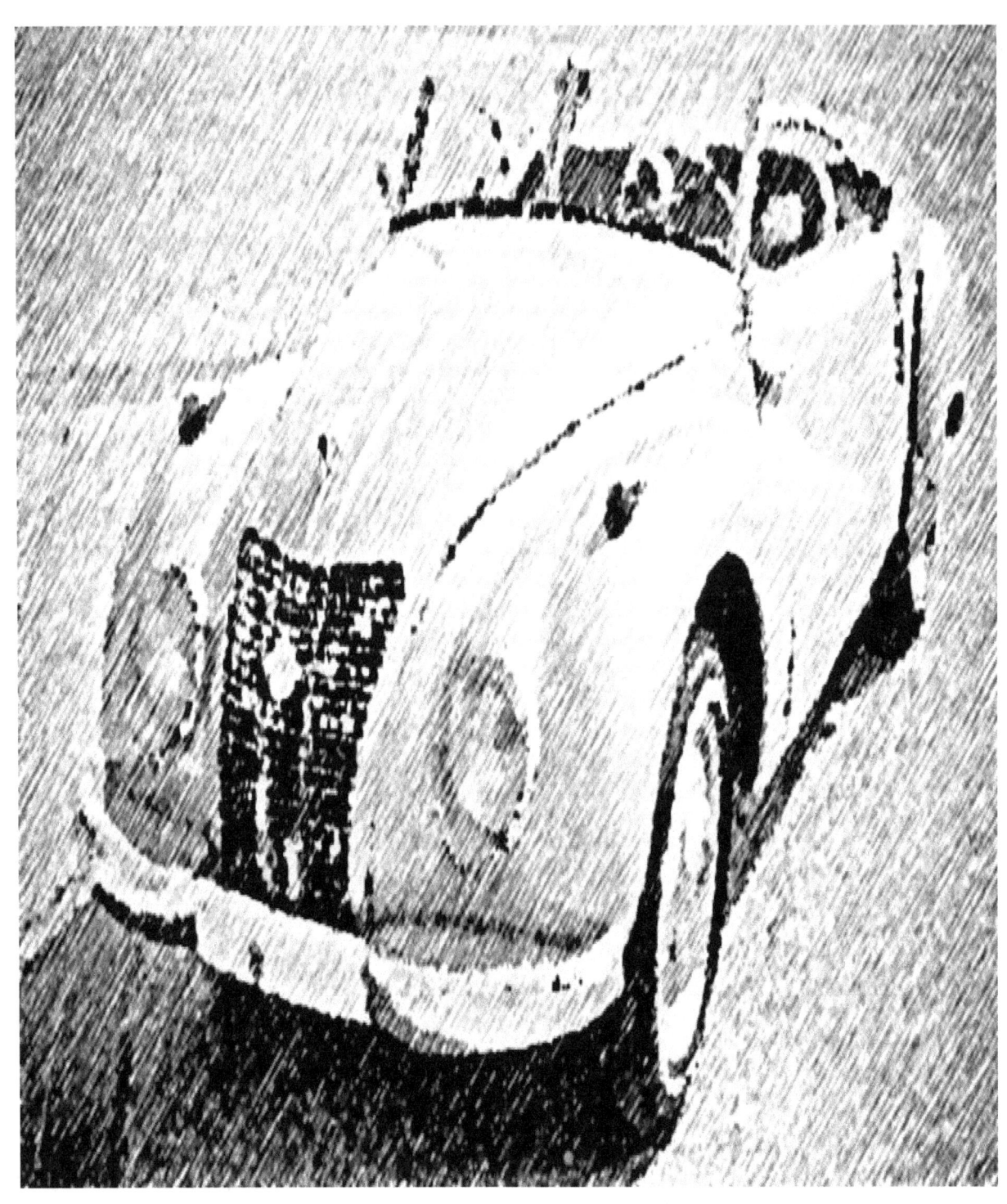

This page is intended for note taking

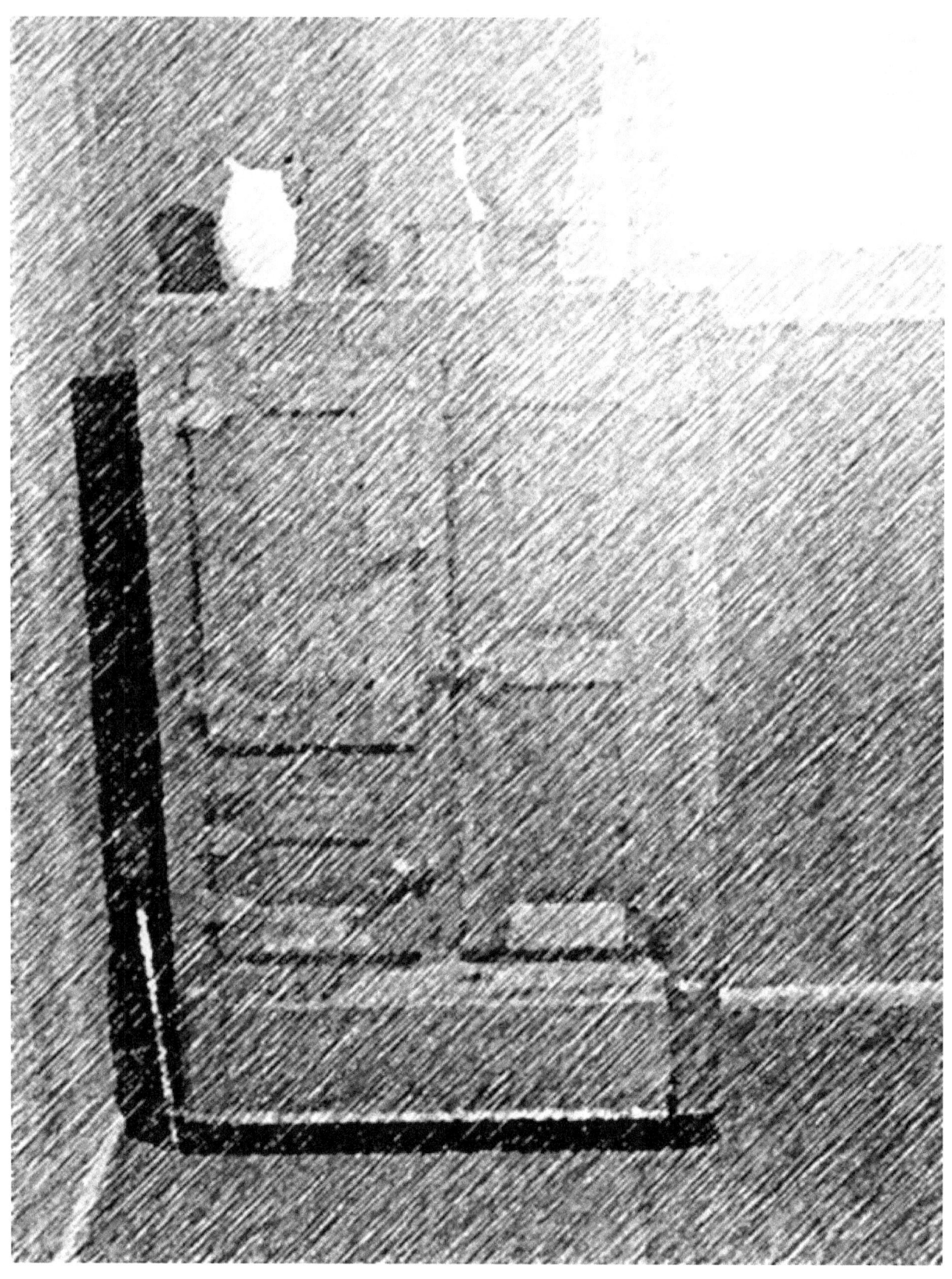

MEDICATION REMINDER

AM 1 X Daily	PM 2 X Daily	SUPPLEMENTS	NOTES

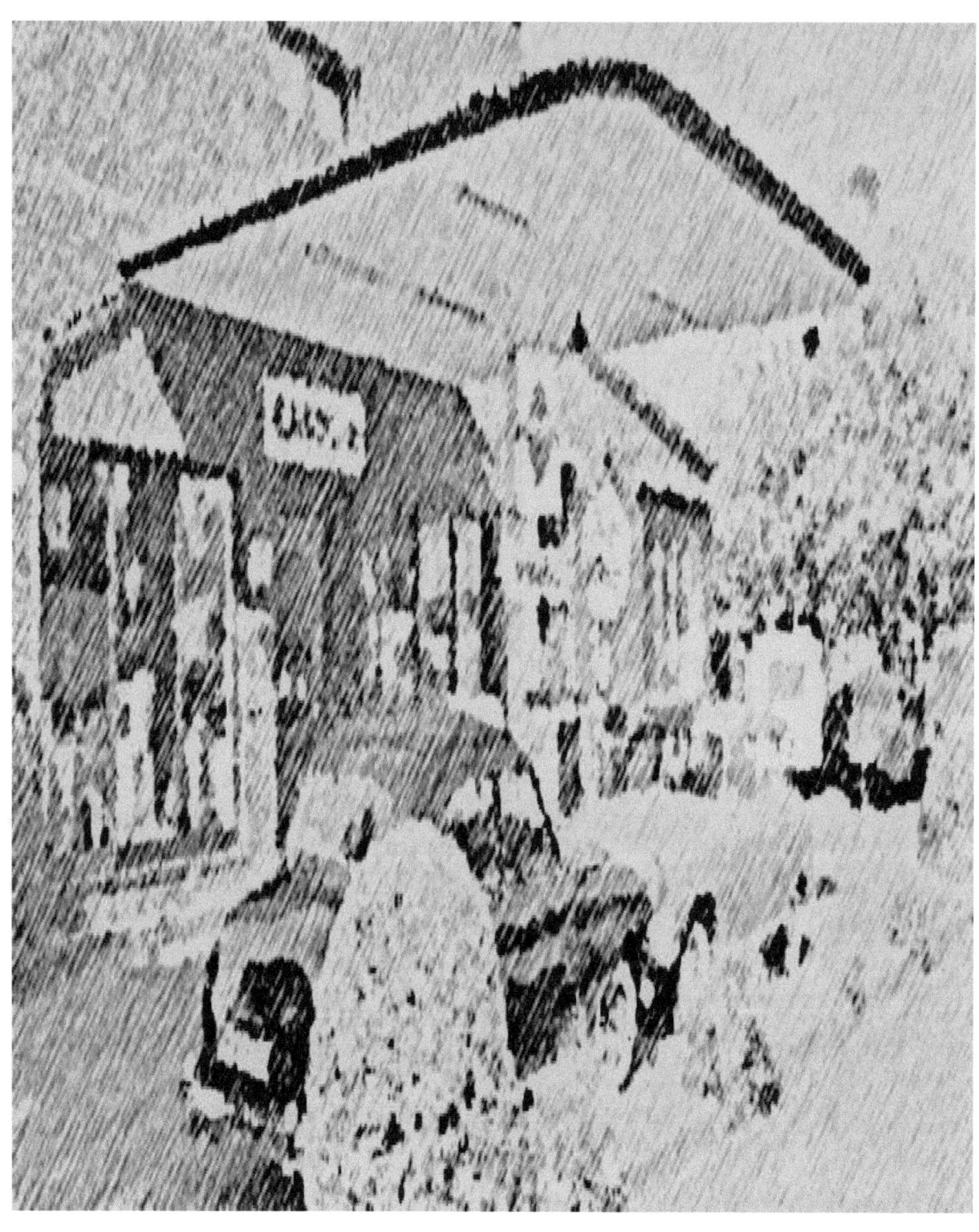

This page Is intended for note taking

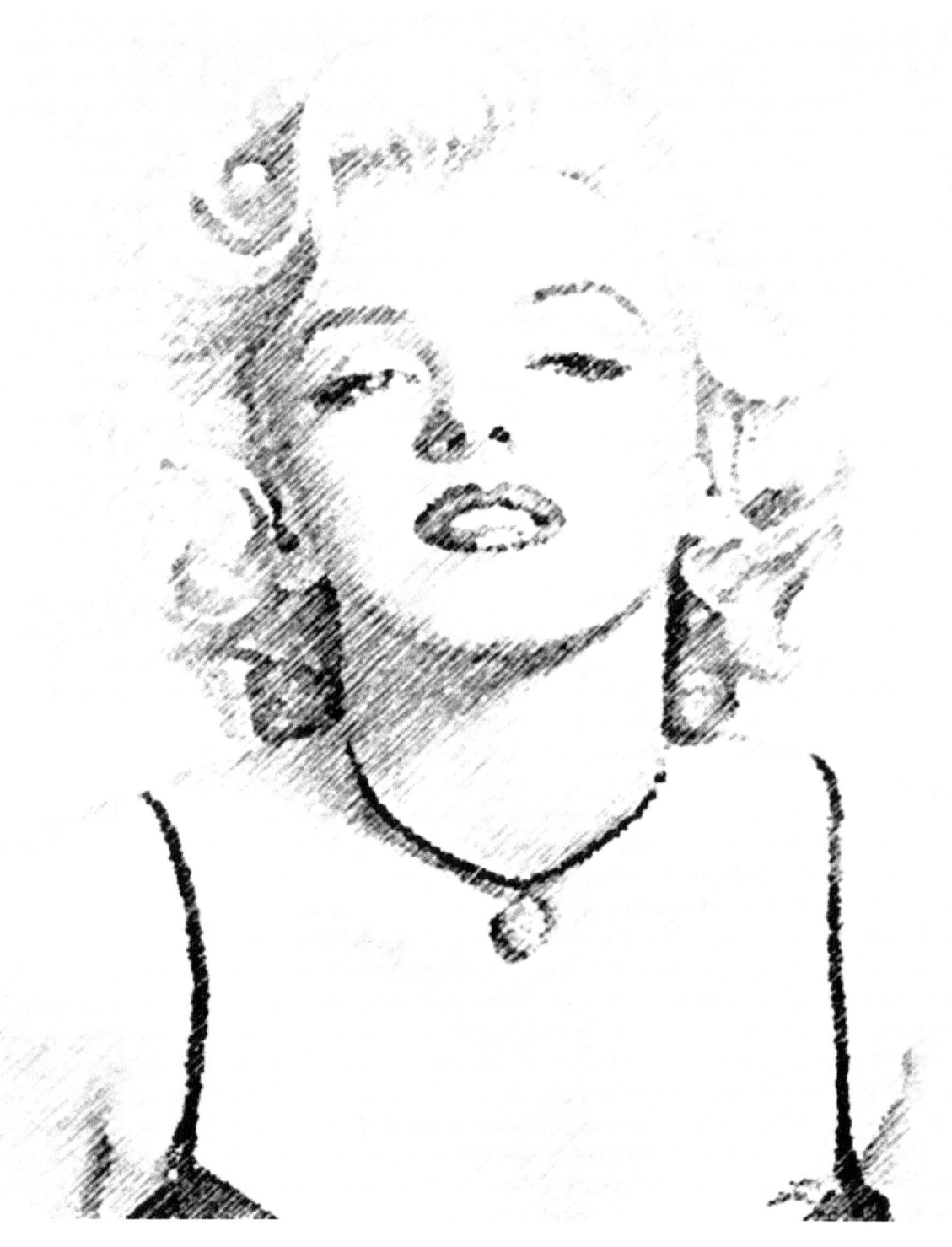

MEDICATION REMINDER

AM 1 X Daily	PM 2 X Daily	SUPPLEMENTS	NOTES

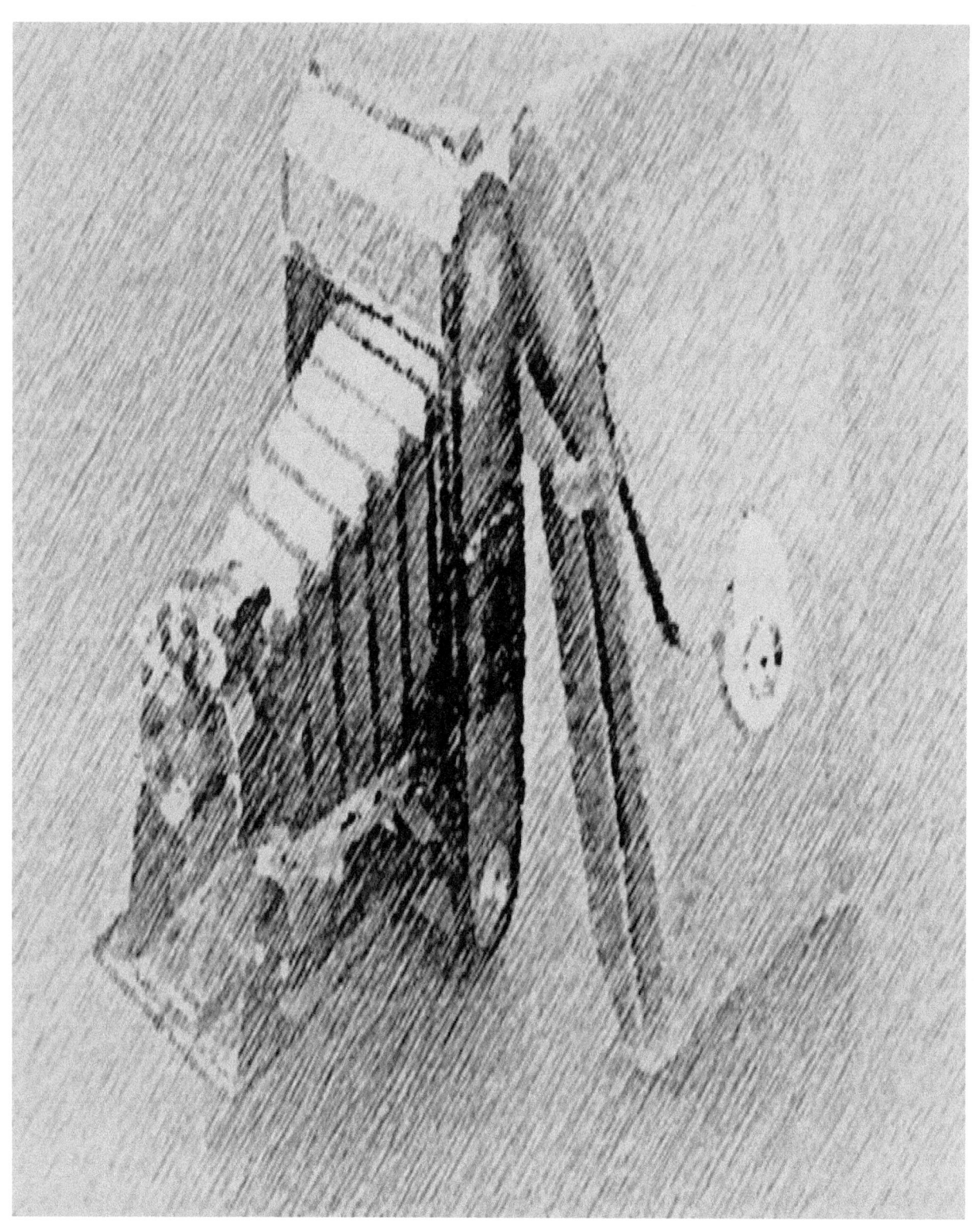

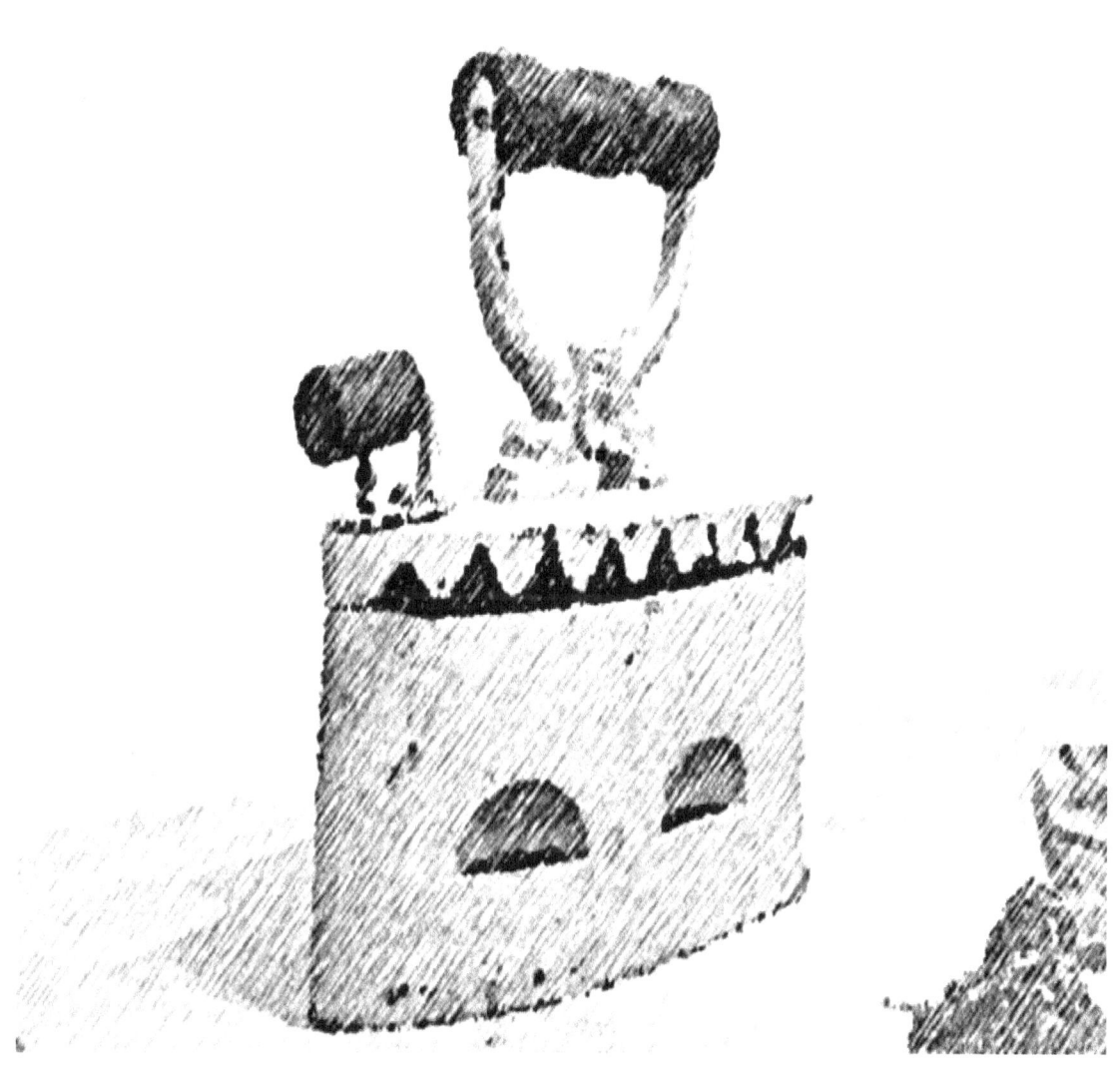

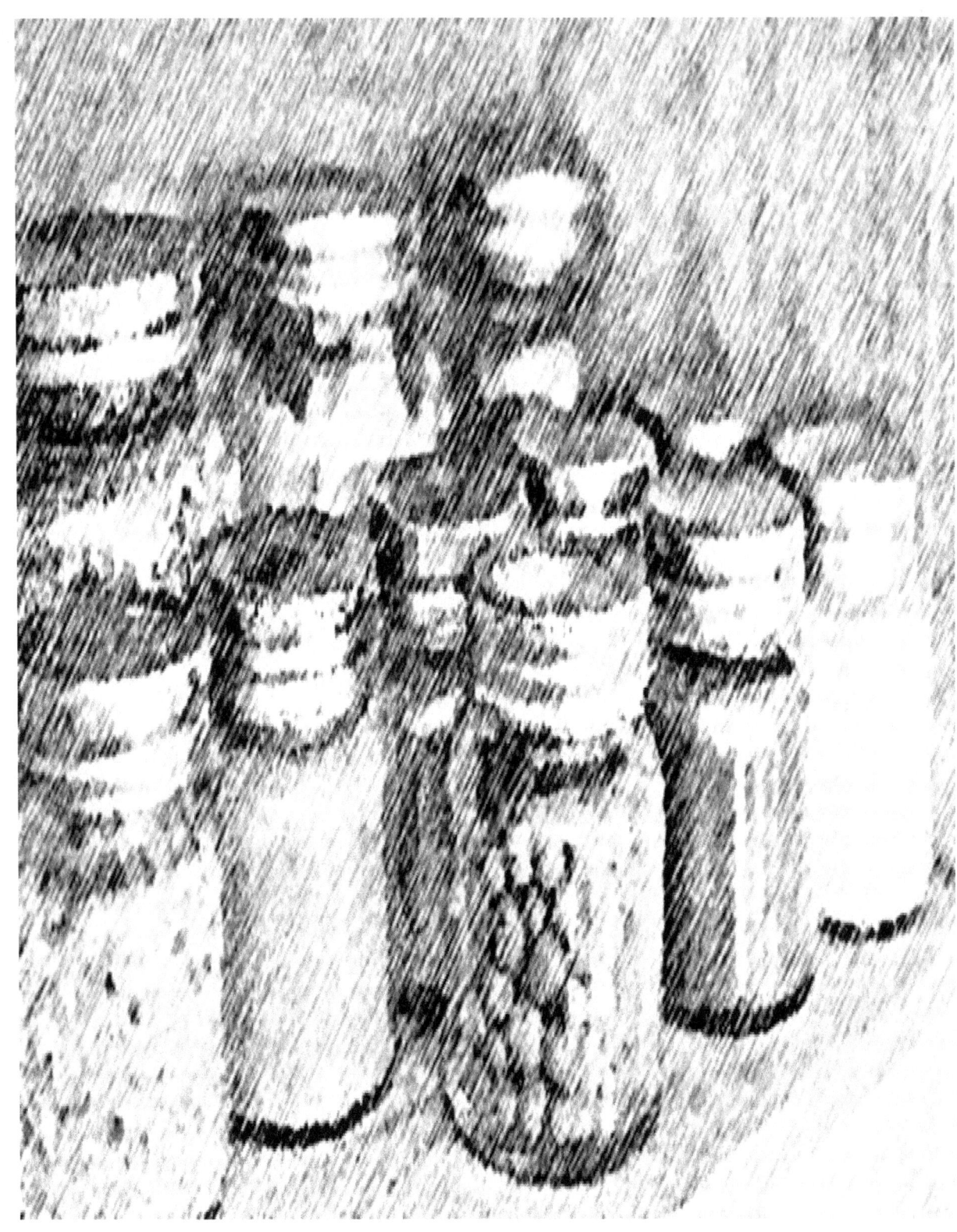

MEDICATION REMINDER

AM 1 X Daily	PM 2 X Daily	Supplements	Notes

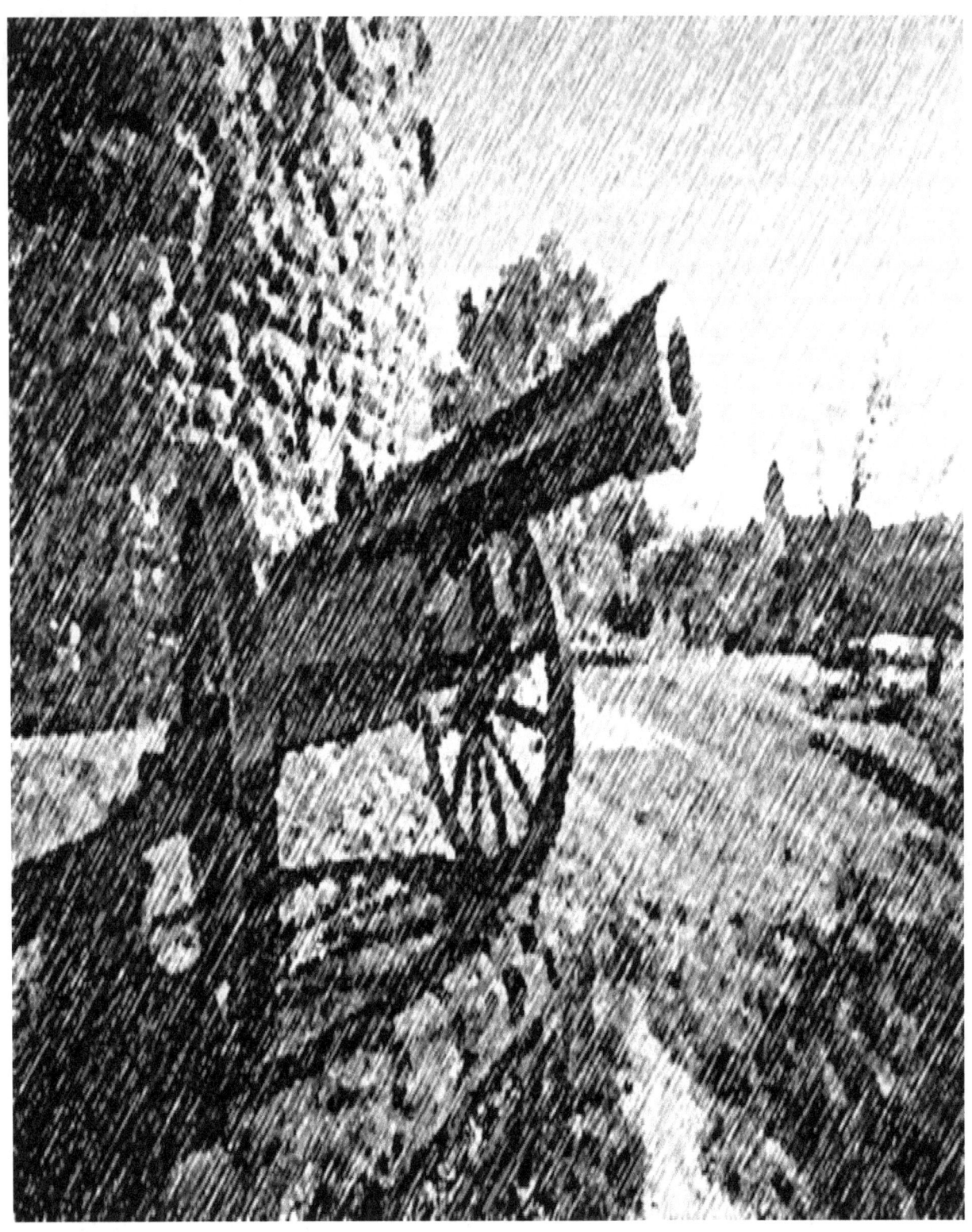

This page is intended for note taking

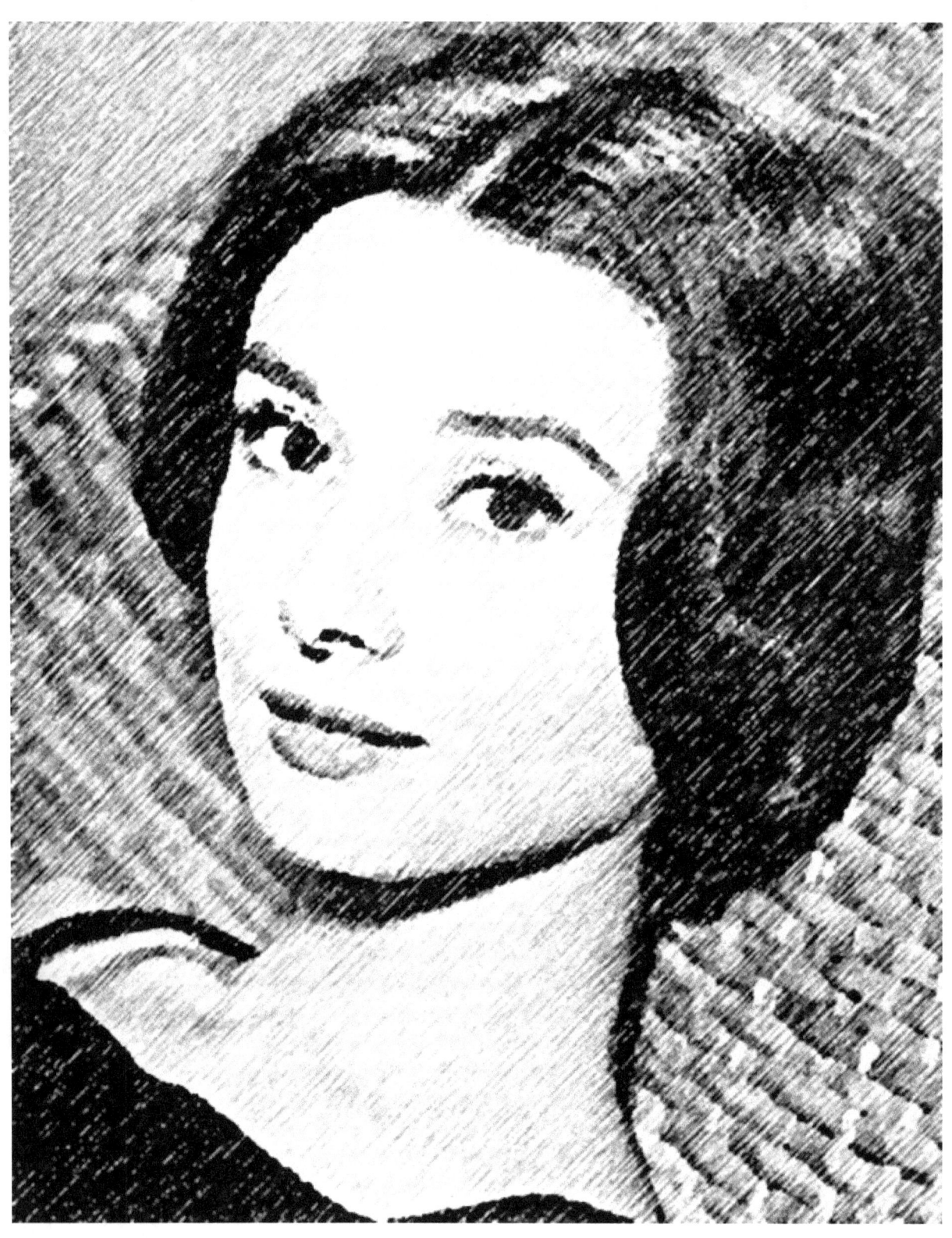

MEDICATION REMINDER

AM 1 X Daily	PM 2 X Daily	Supplements	Notes

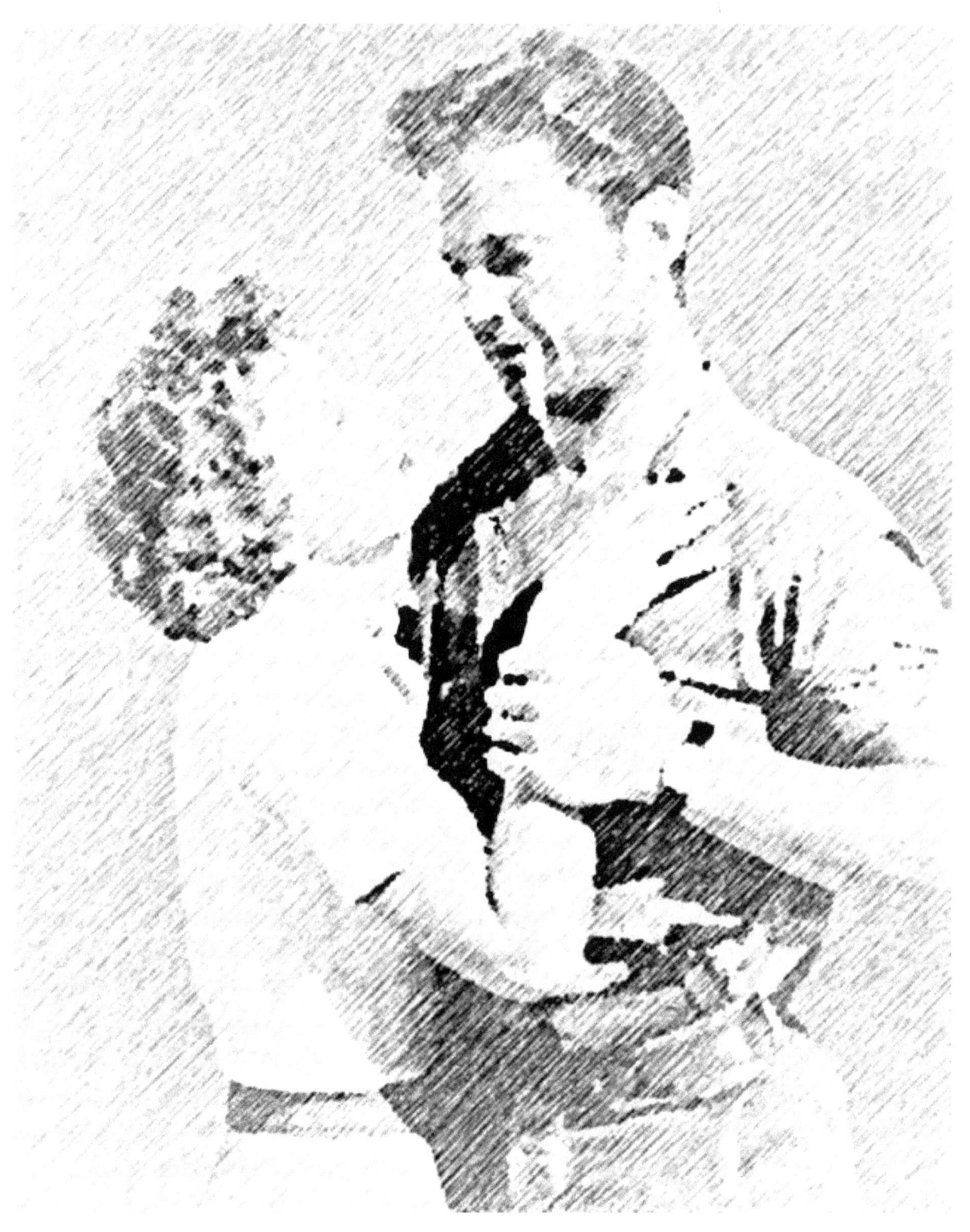

This page is intended for note taking

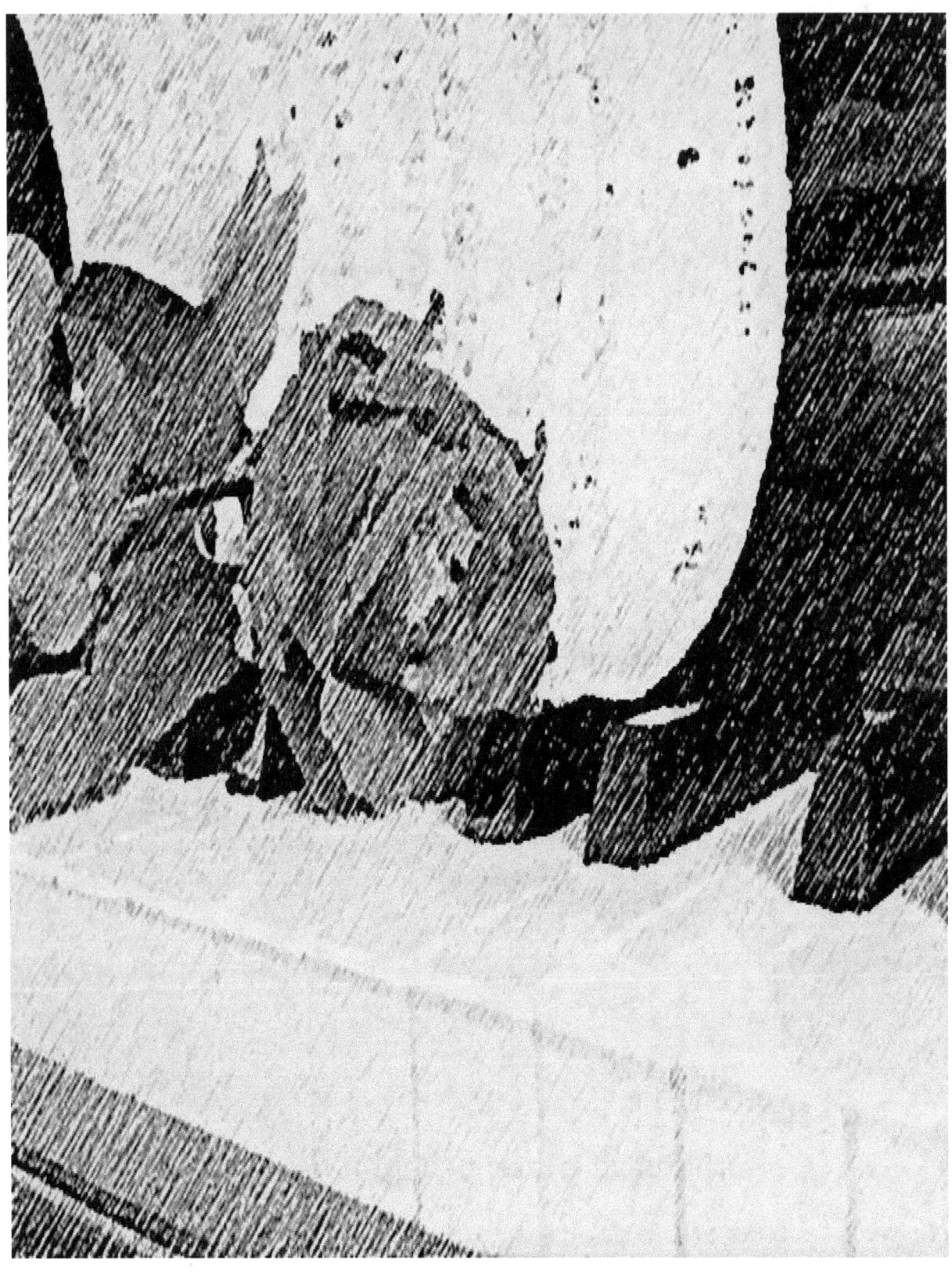

MEDICATION REMINDER

AM 1X Daily	PM 2 X Daily	SUPPLEMENTS	NOTES

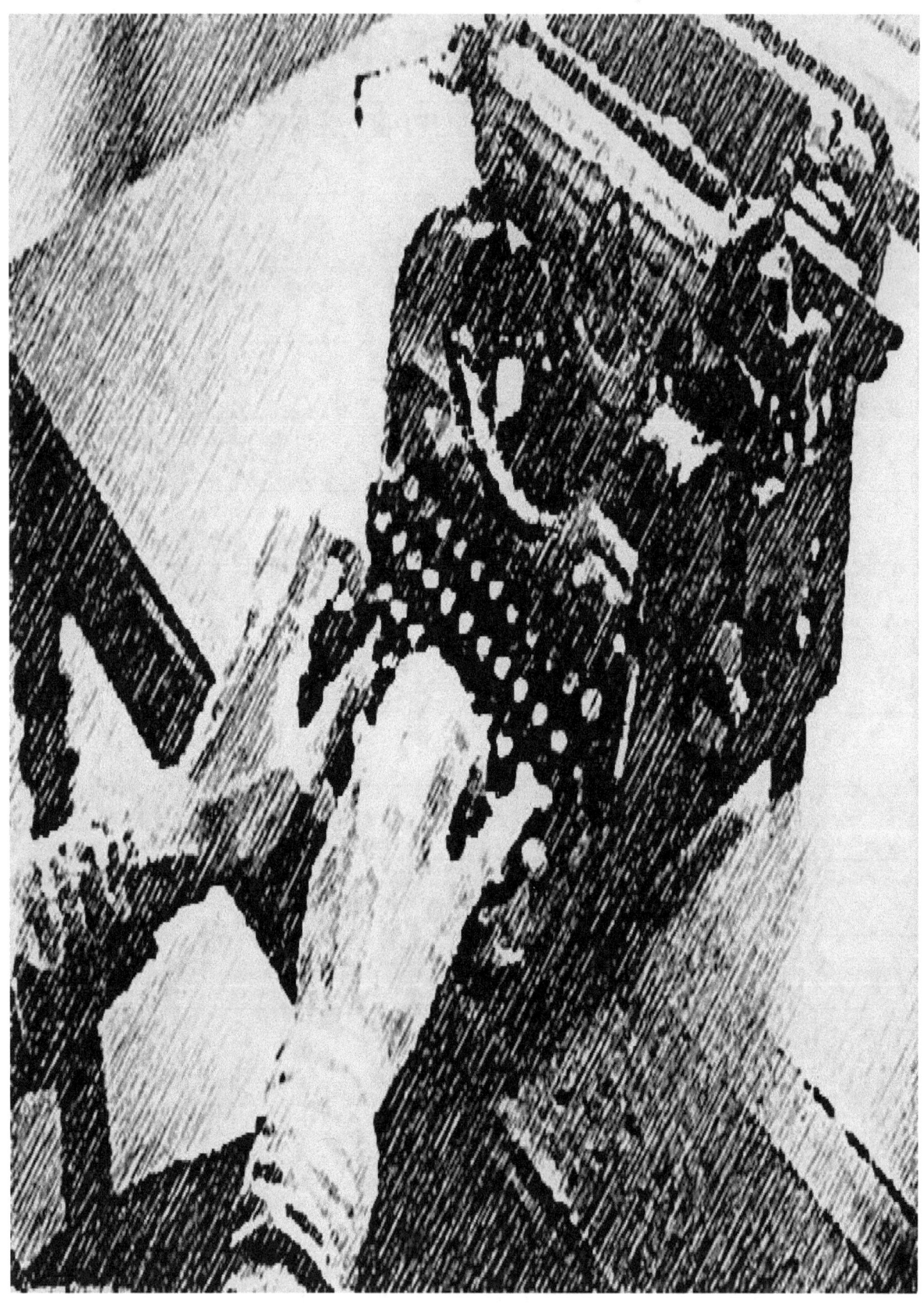

CIRCLE 8 DAILY MUST DO'S

BATHING/SHOWERING	SING IN AN OPERA
HORSEBACK RIDING	CLIMB THE STAIRS
GO TO THE ZOO	DRIVE ALONG THE BEACH
BRUSH YOUR TEETH	SKI THE SLOPES
EAT THREE NUTRITIOUS MEALS DAILY	TRANSFER FROM CHAIR TO COUCH
GO JOGGING AT THE PARK	SIGHT SEEING ON A CRUISE SHIP
HAVE GOOD GROOMING HABITS	USE THE RESTROOM
FEED SOME PIGEONS	TAKE A WALK

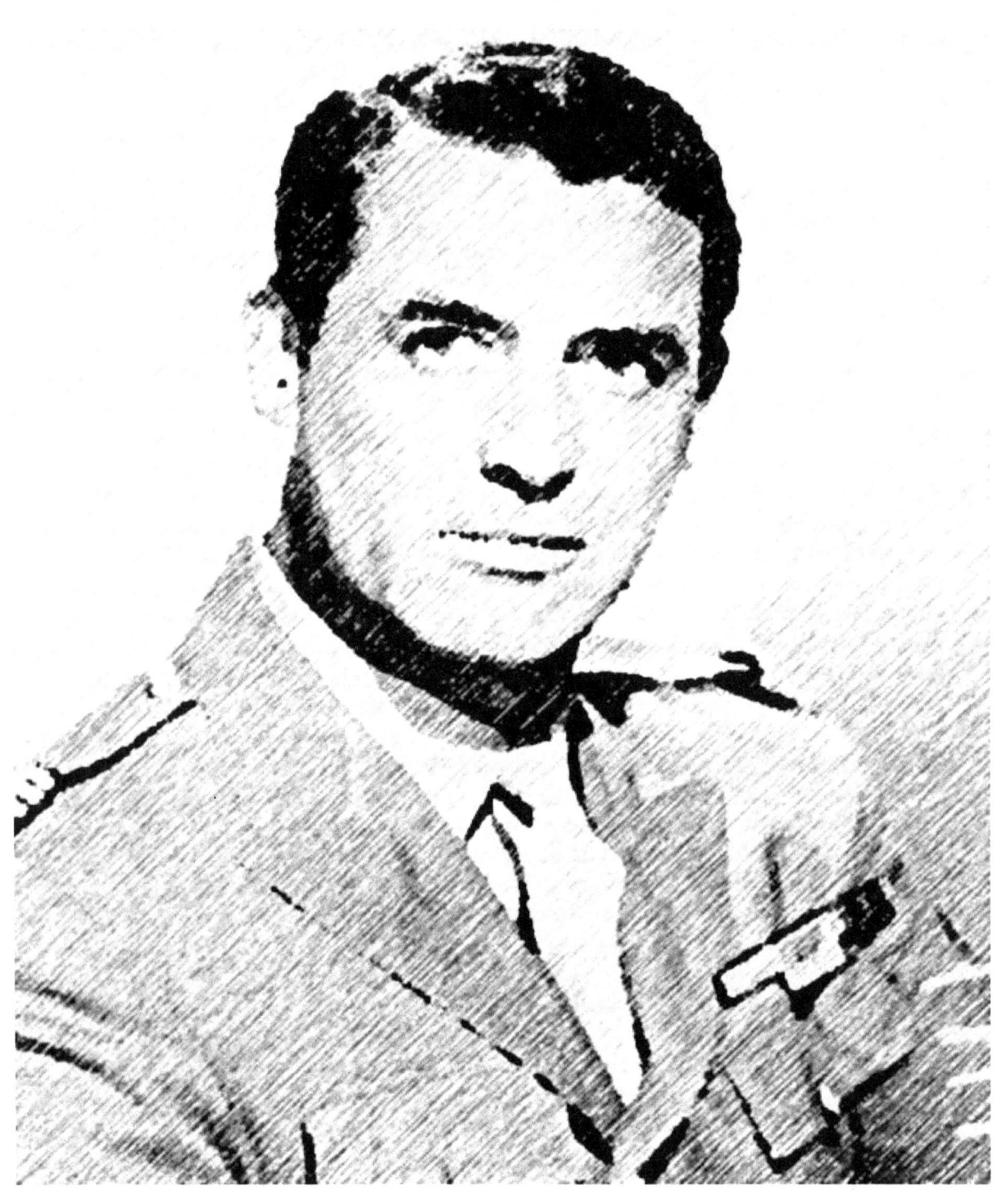

This page is intended for note taking

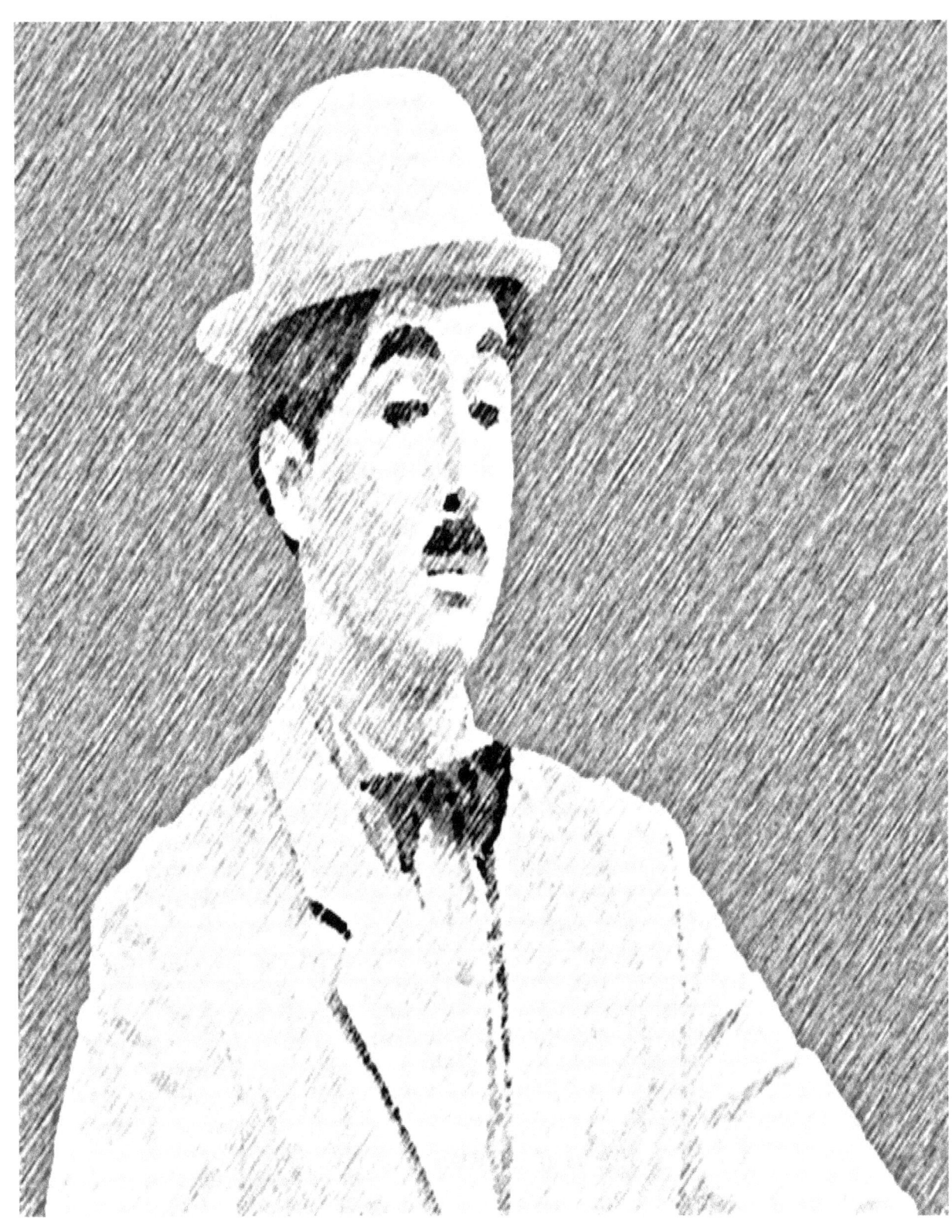

MEDICATION REMINDER

AM 1 X Daily	PM 2 X Daily	SUPPLEMENTS	NOTES

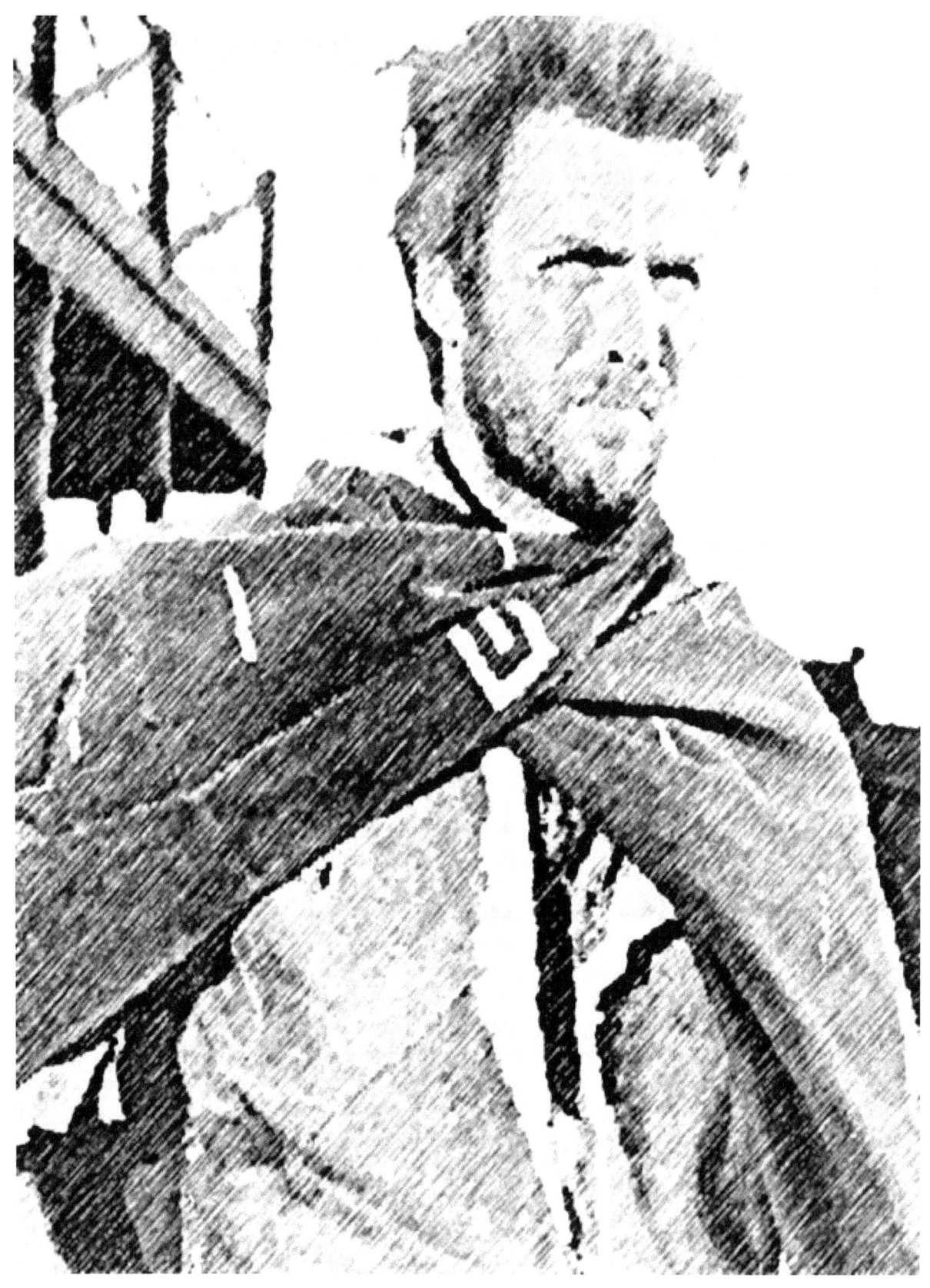

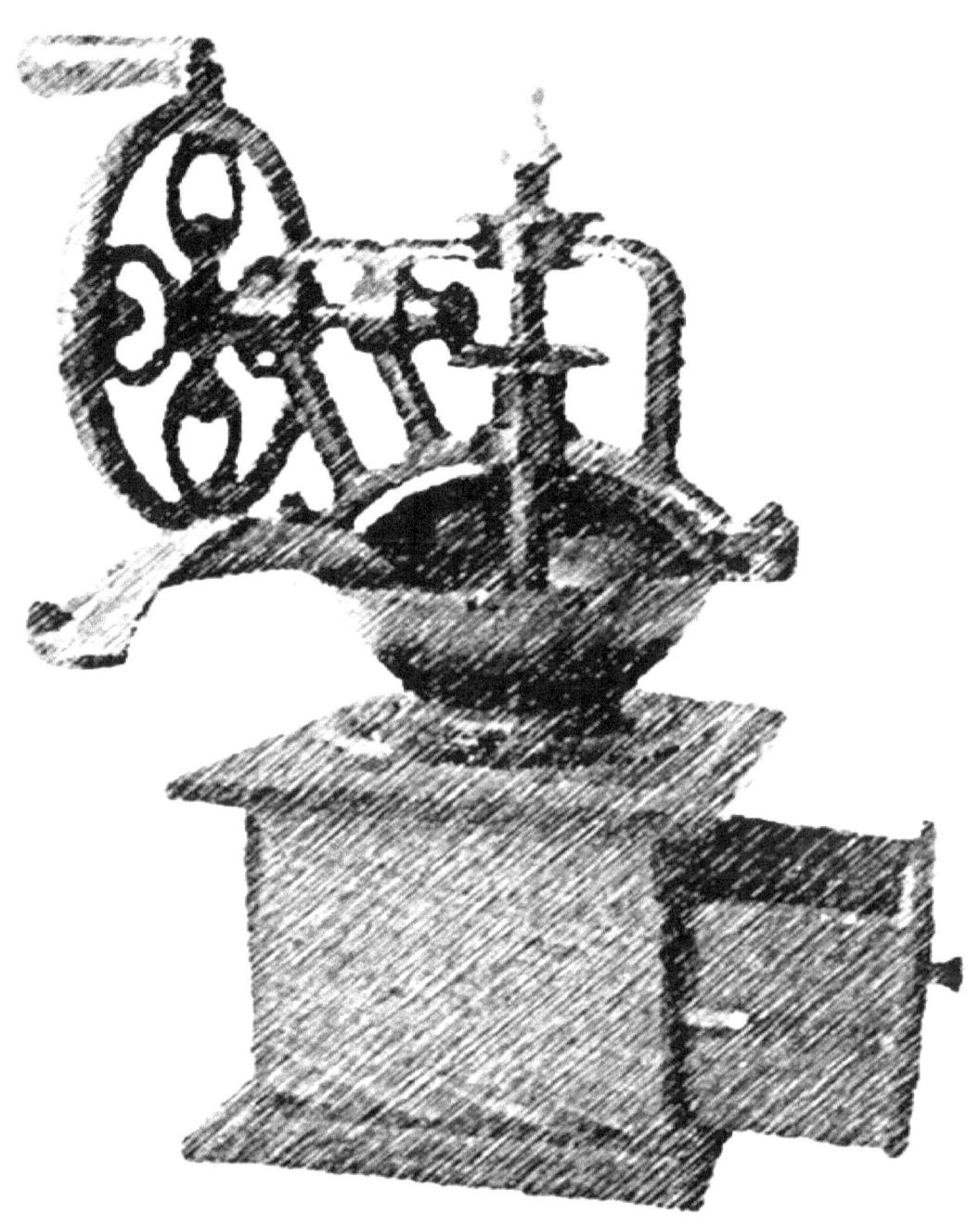

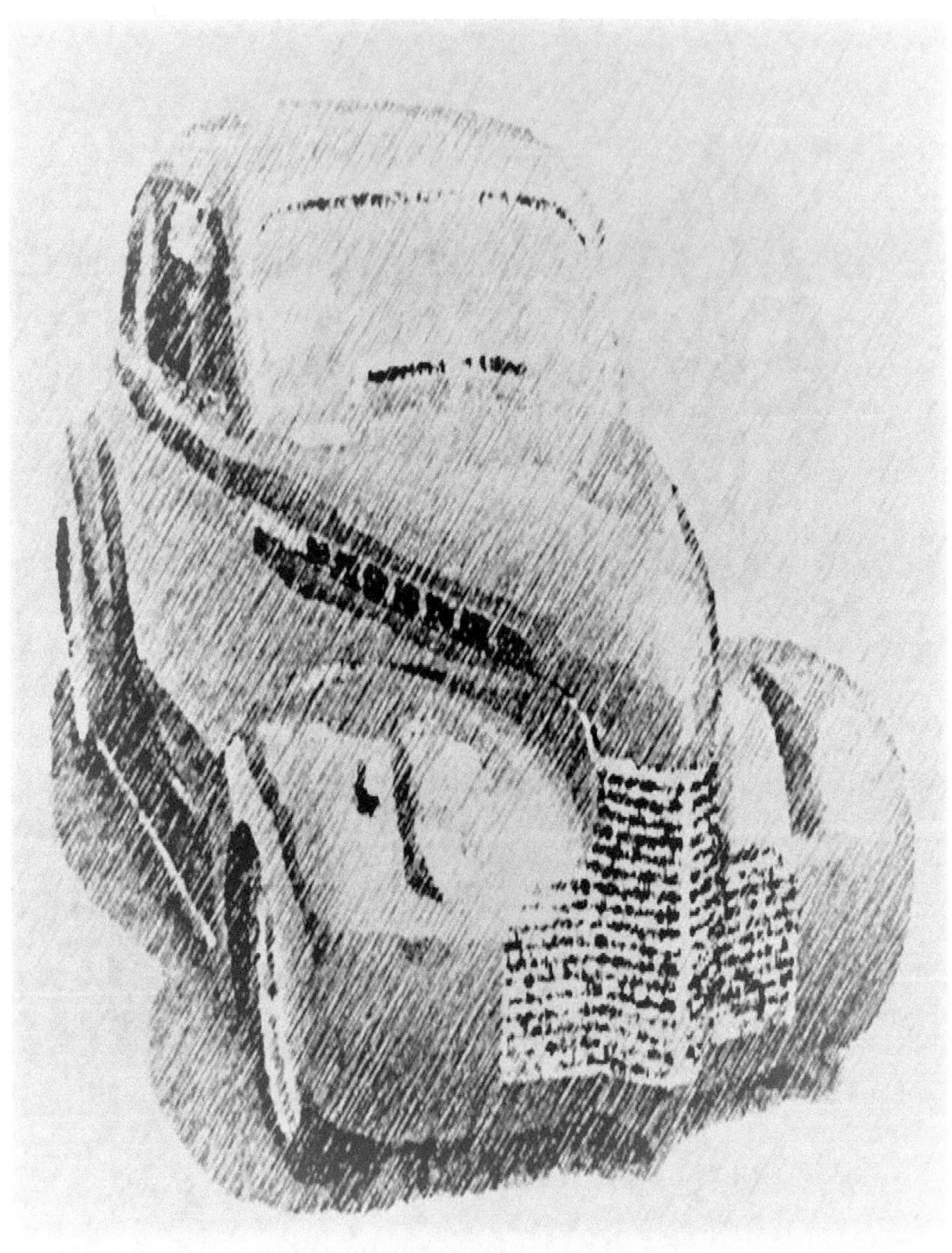

MEDICATION REMINDER

AM 1 X Daily	PM 2 X Daily	SUPPLEMENTS	NOTES

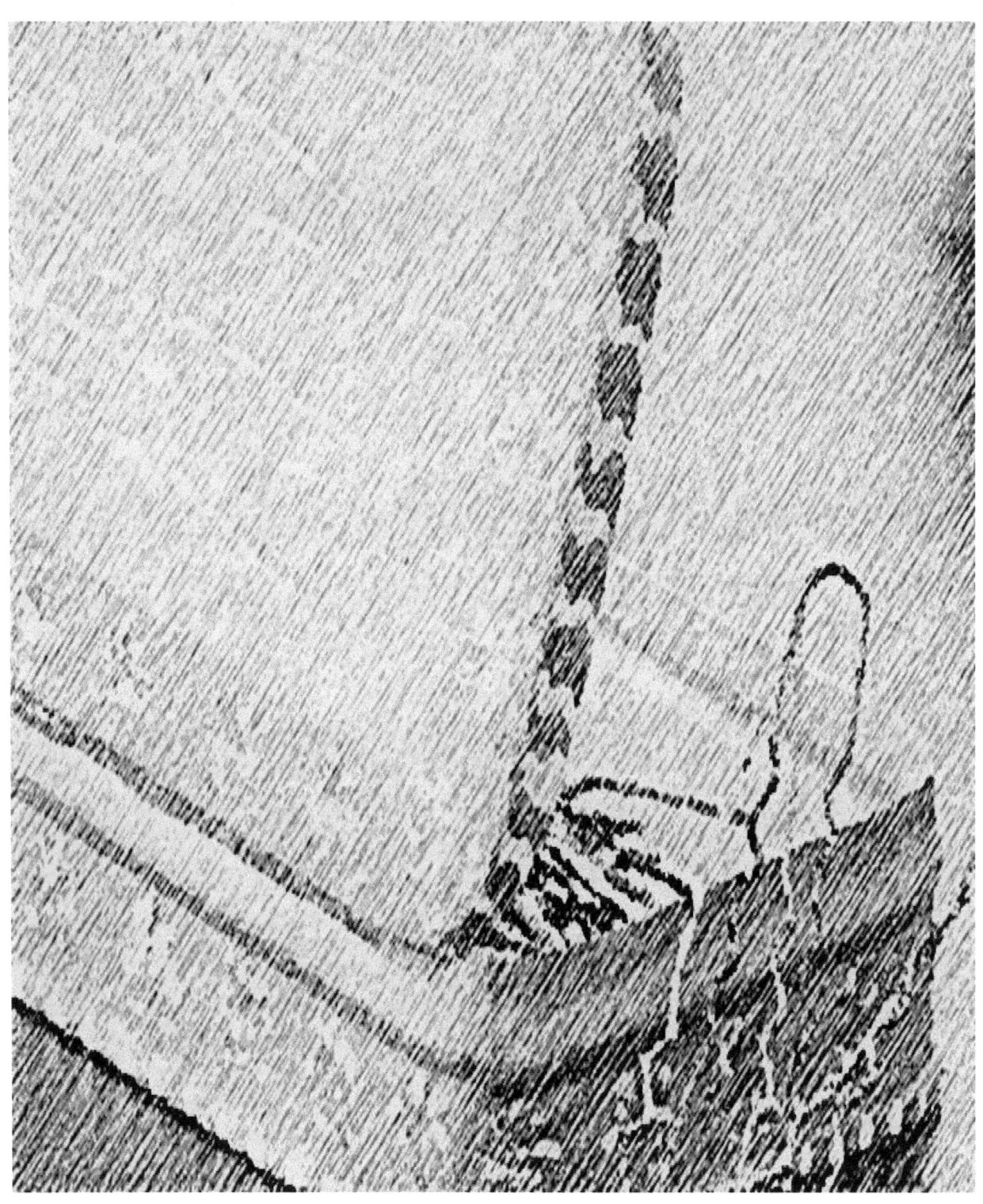

This page is intended for note taking

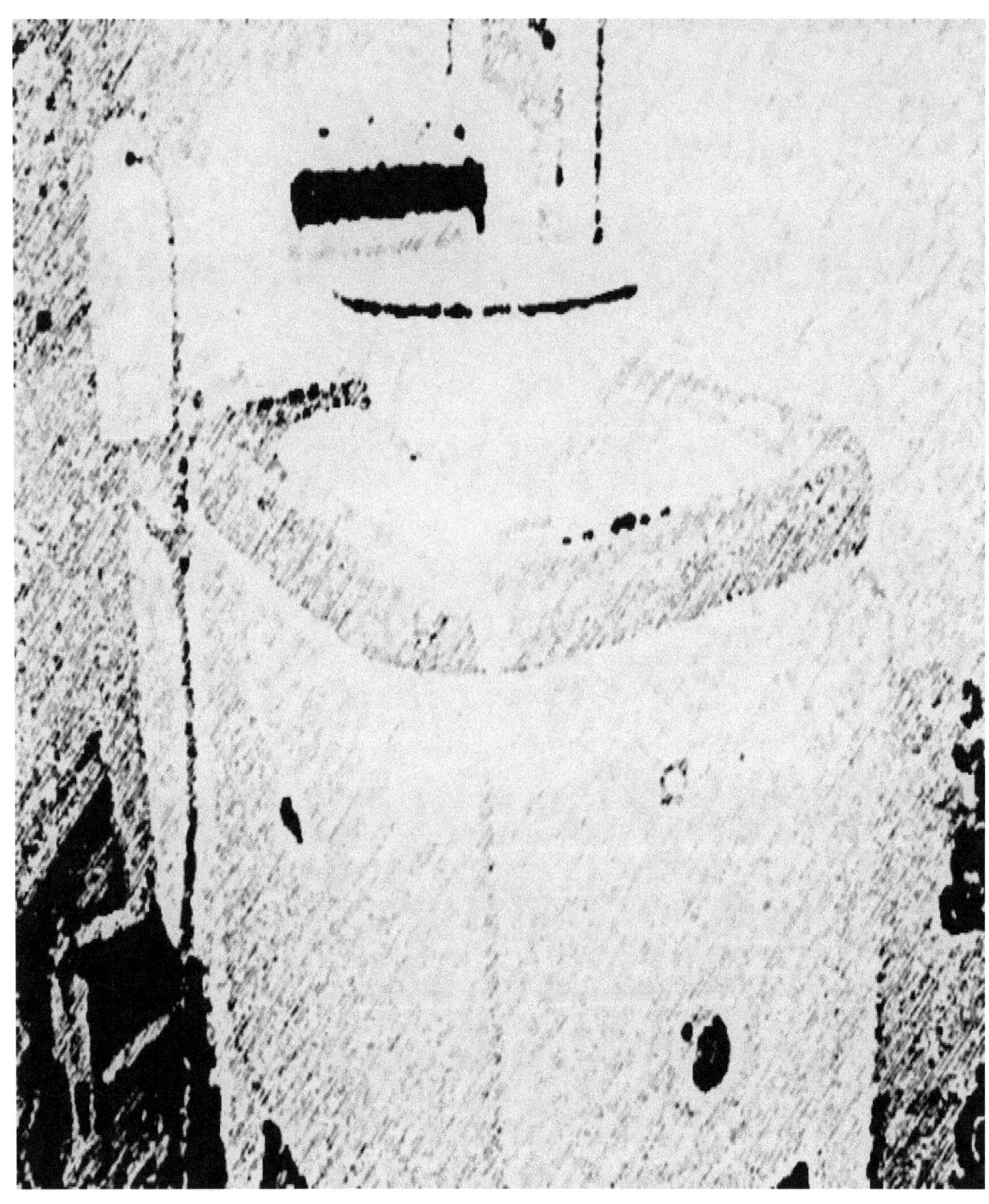

MEDICATION REMINDER

AM 1 X Daily	PM 2 X Daily	SUPPLEMENTS	NOTES

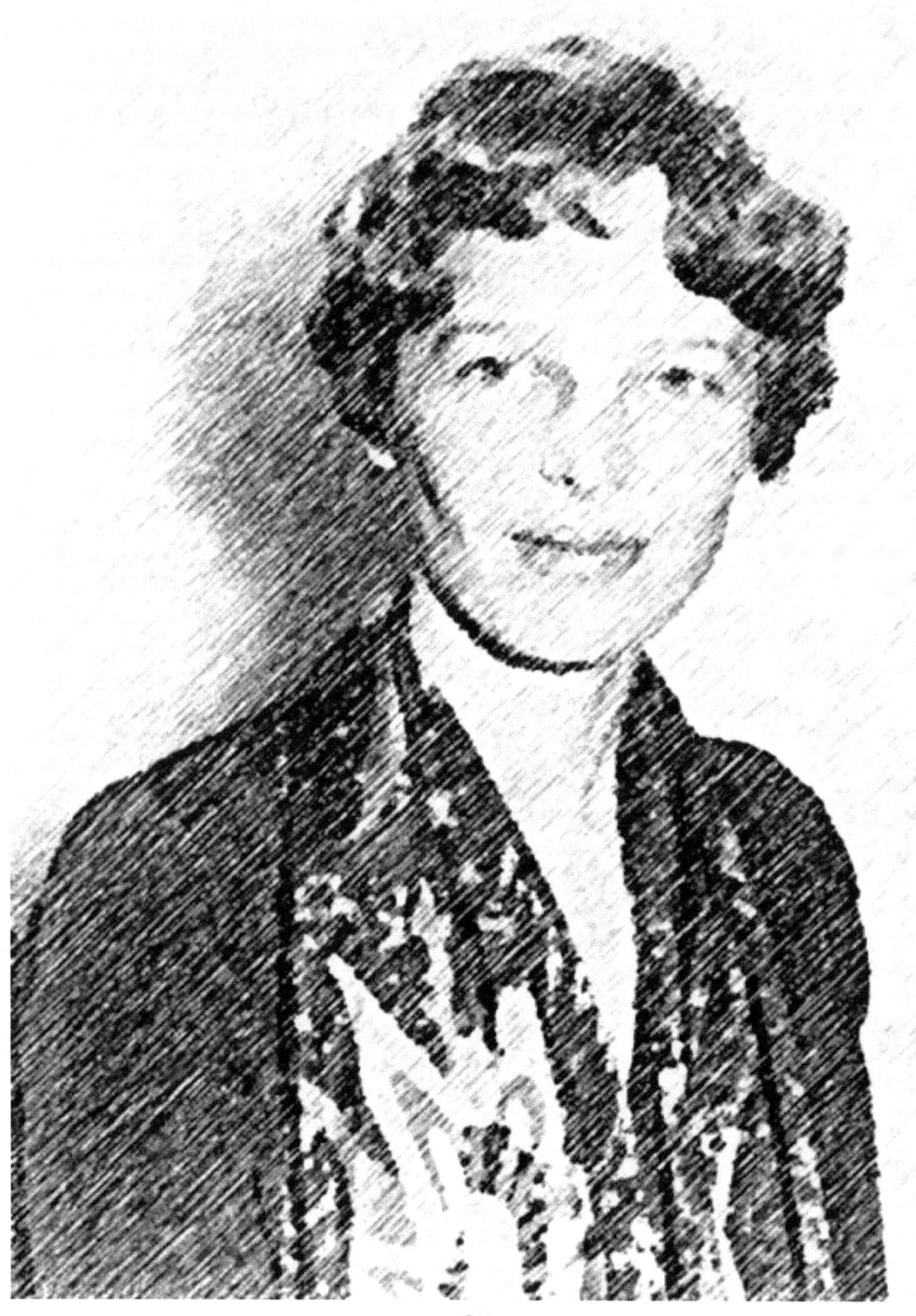

This page is intended for note taking

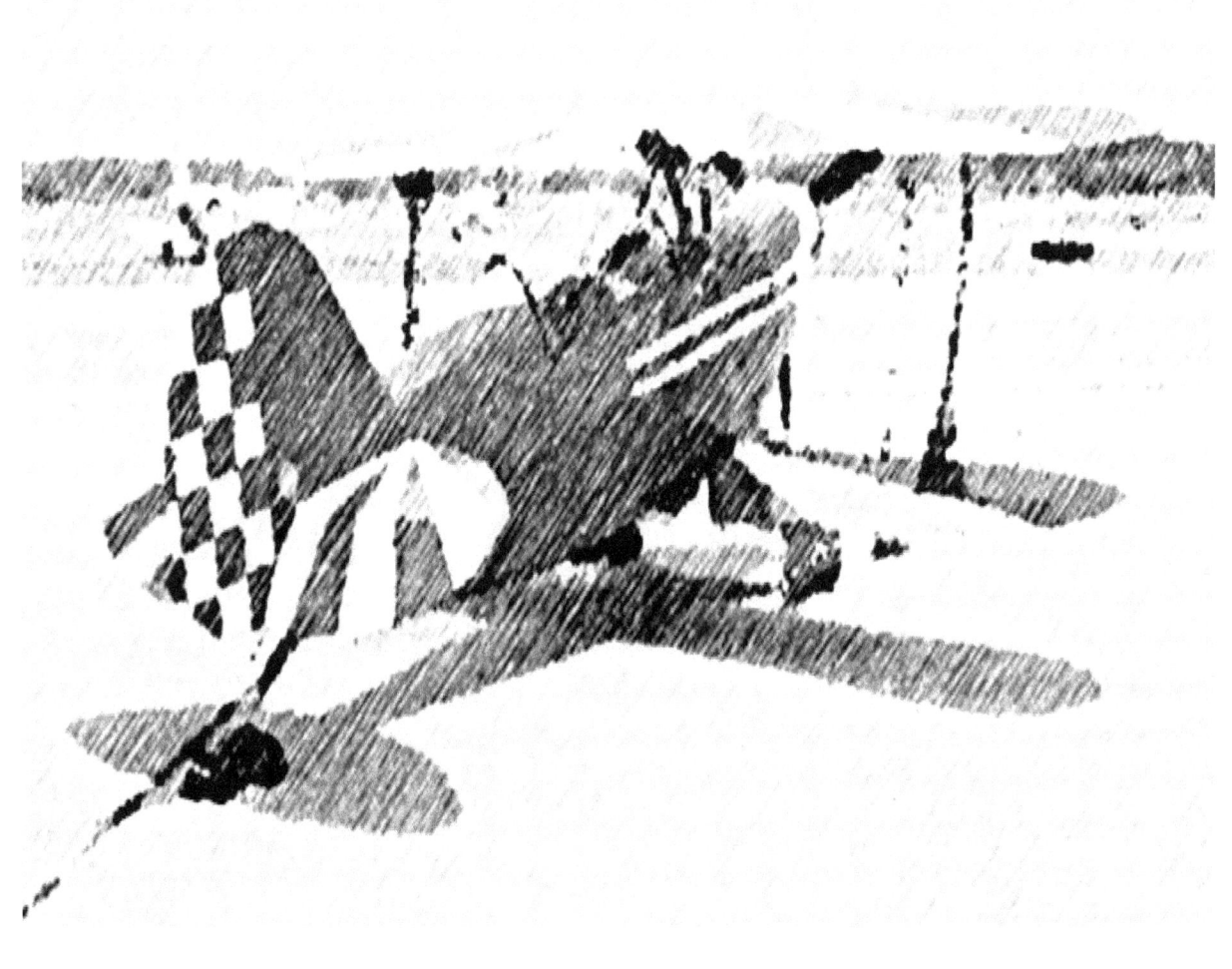

MEDICATION REMINDER

AM 1 X Daily	PM 2 X Daily	SUPPLEMENTS	NOTES

This page is intended for note taking

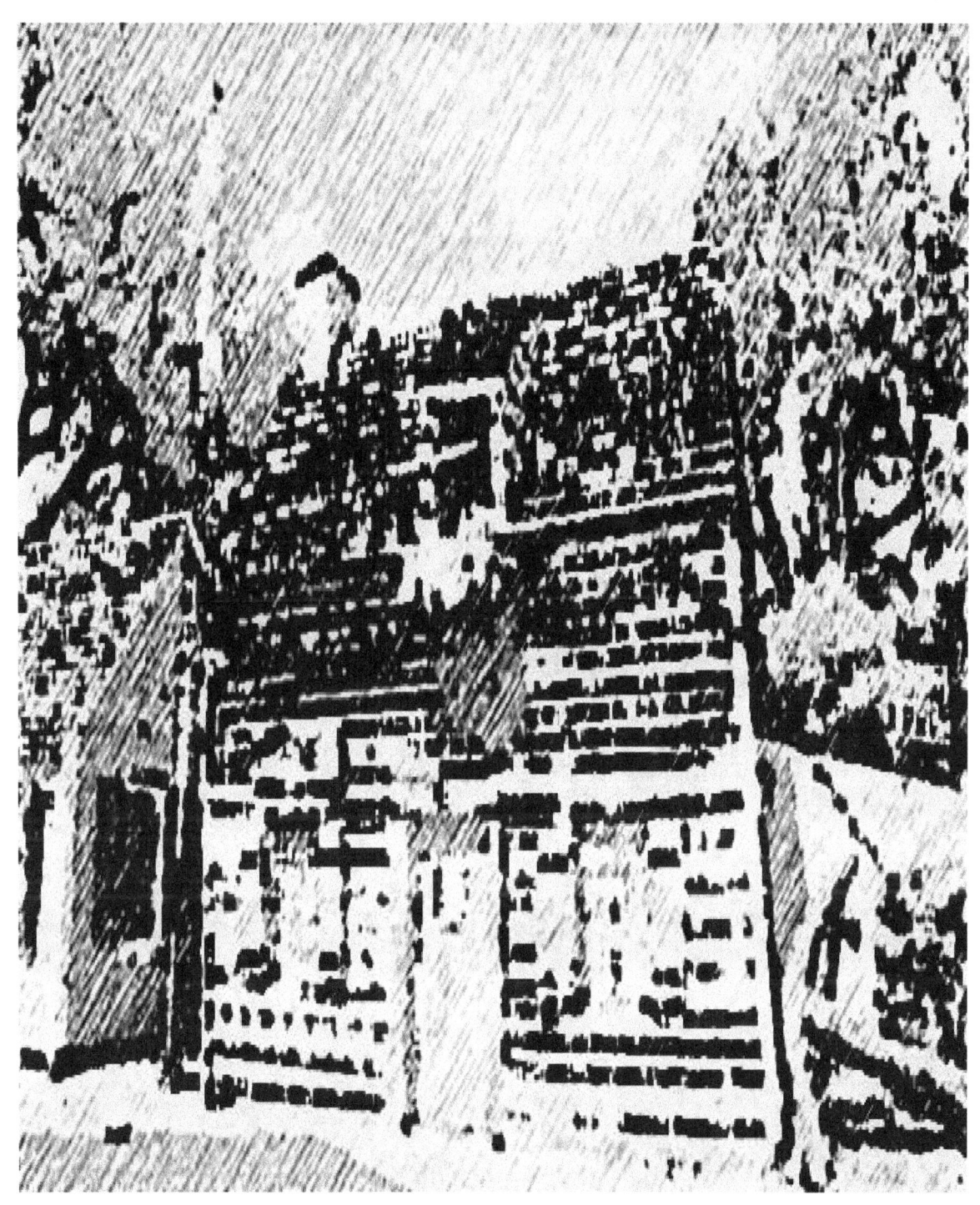

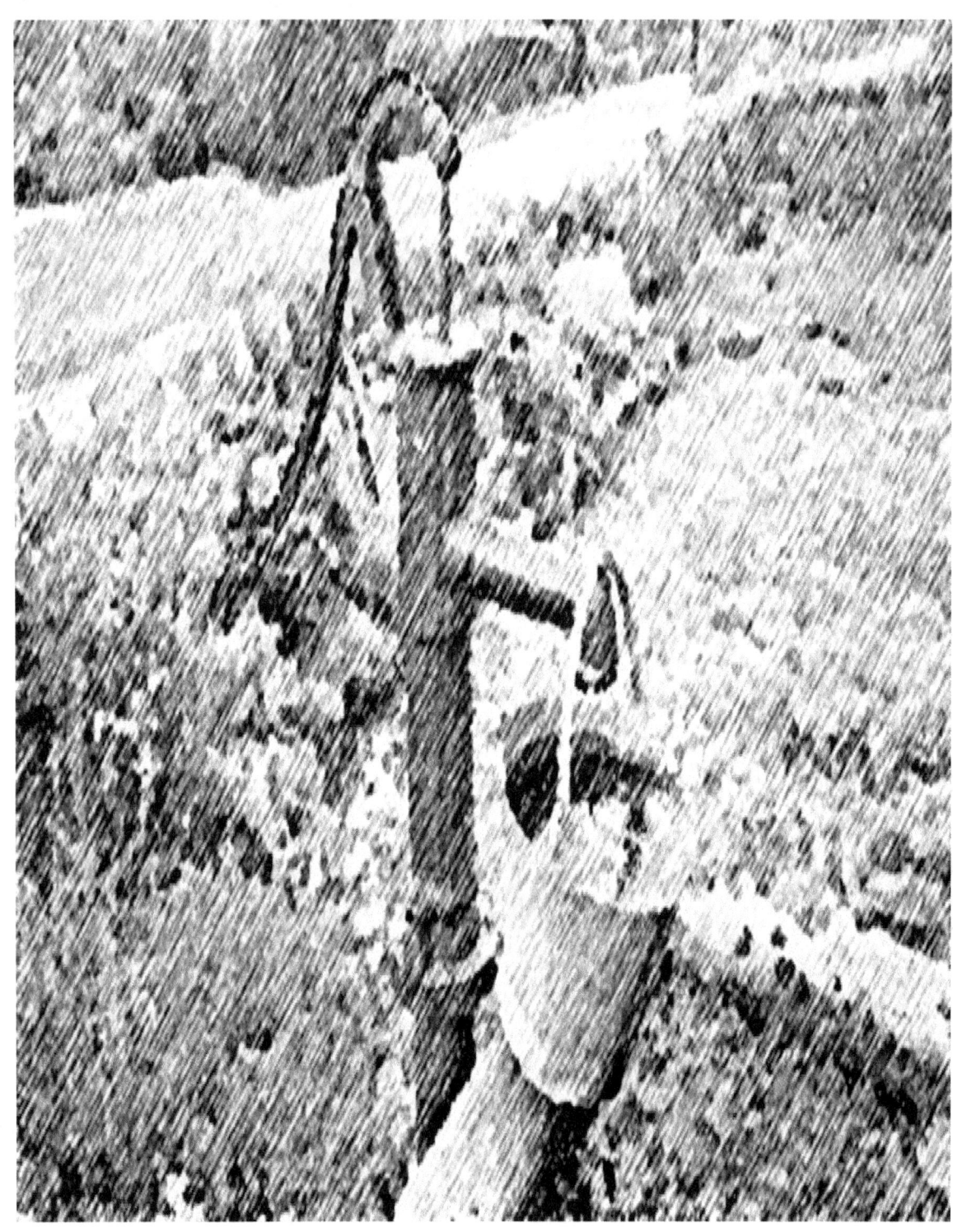

MEDICATION REMINDER

AM 1X Daily	PM 2X Daily	SUPPLEMENTS	NOTES

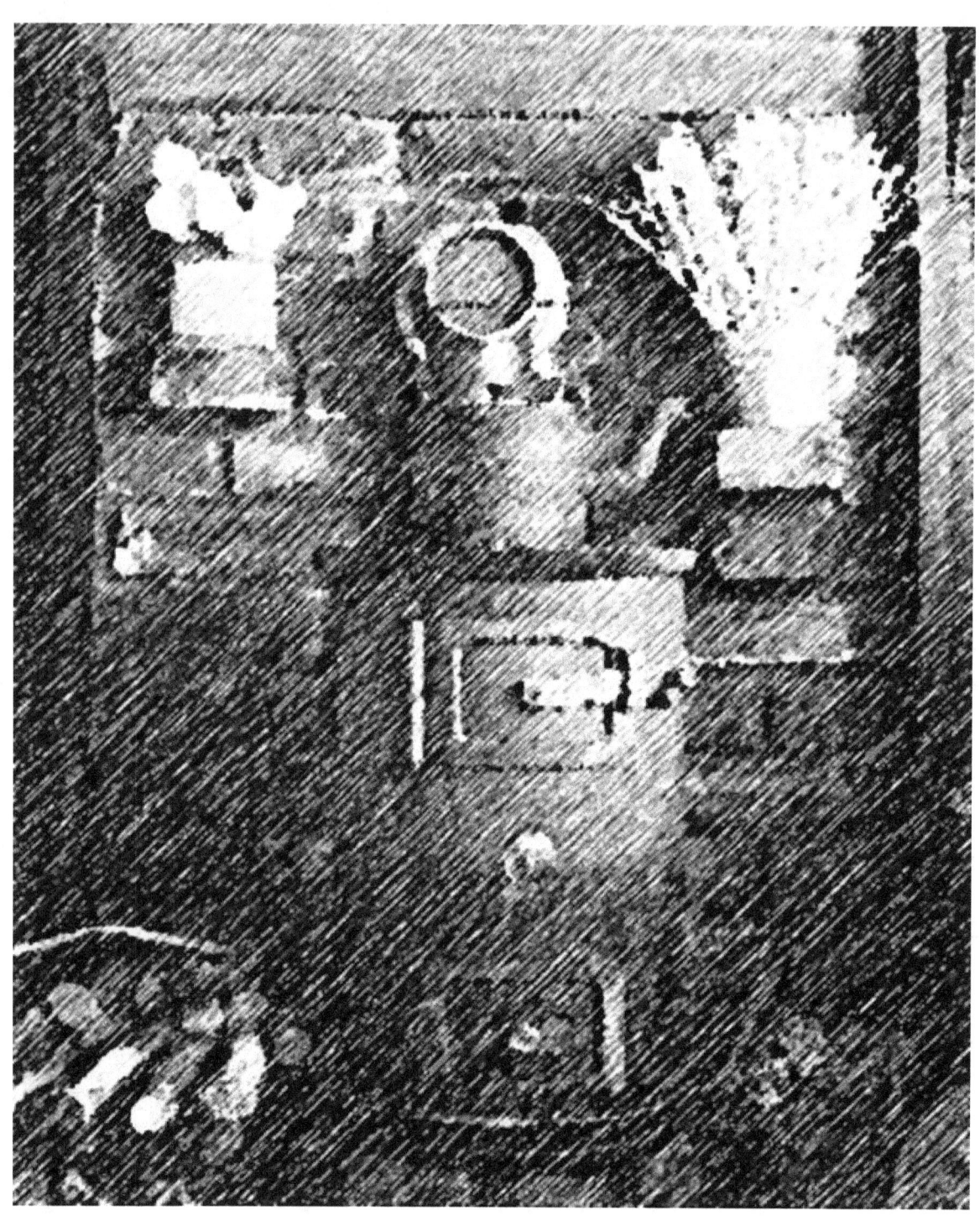

This page is intended for note taking

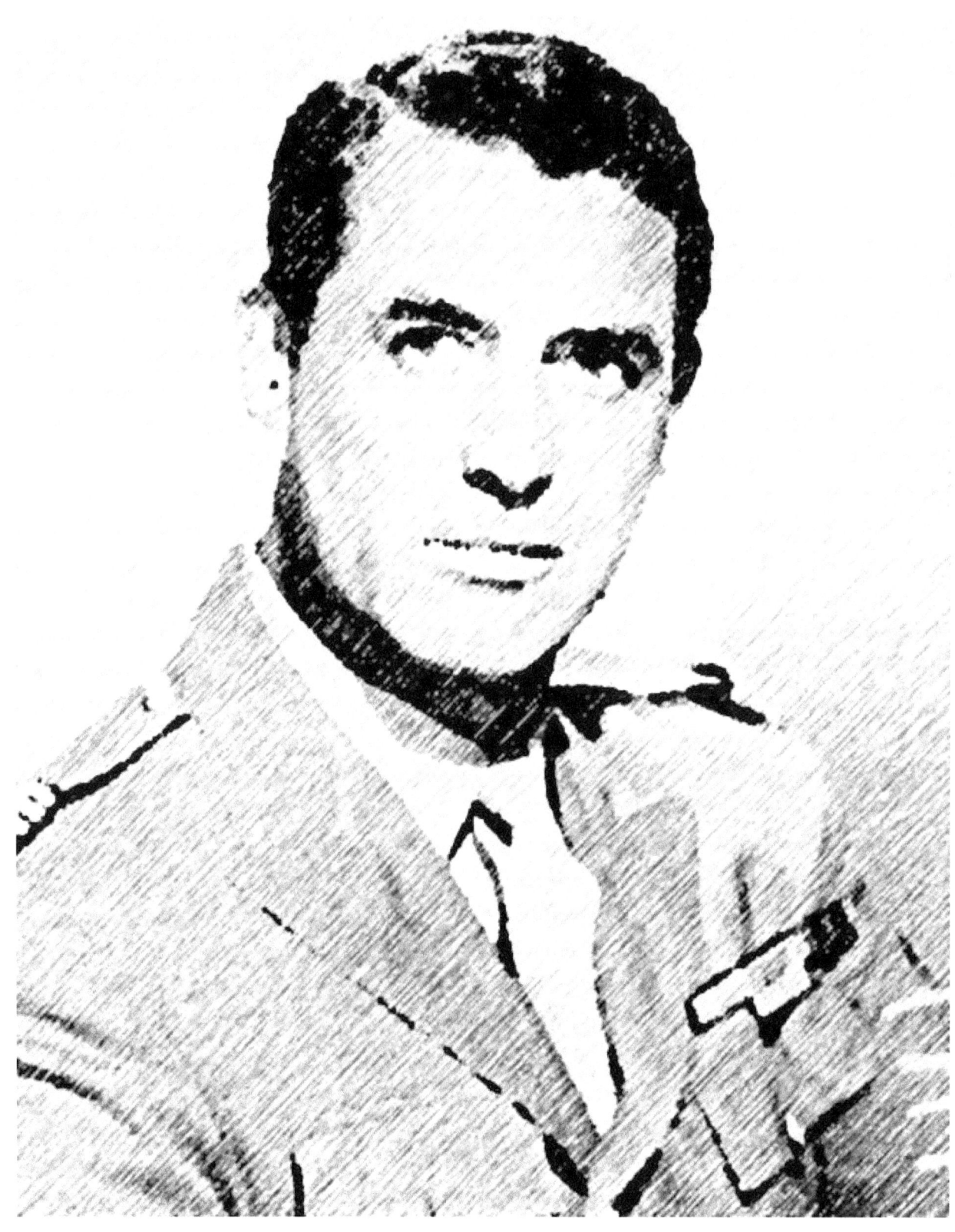

MEDICATION REMINDER

AM 1X Daily	PM 2X Daily	SUPPLEMENTS	NOTES

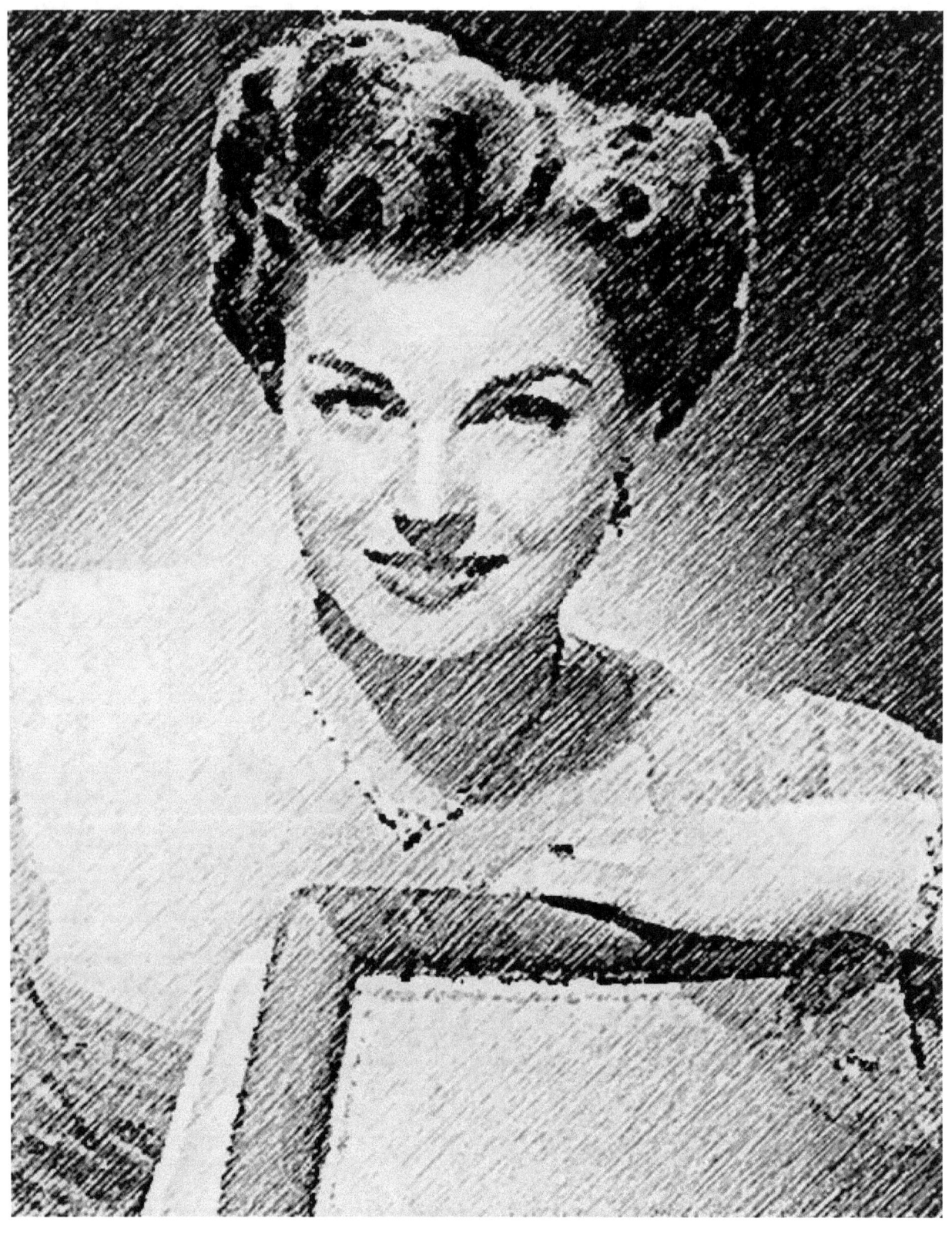

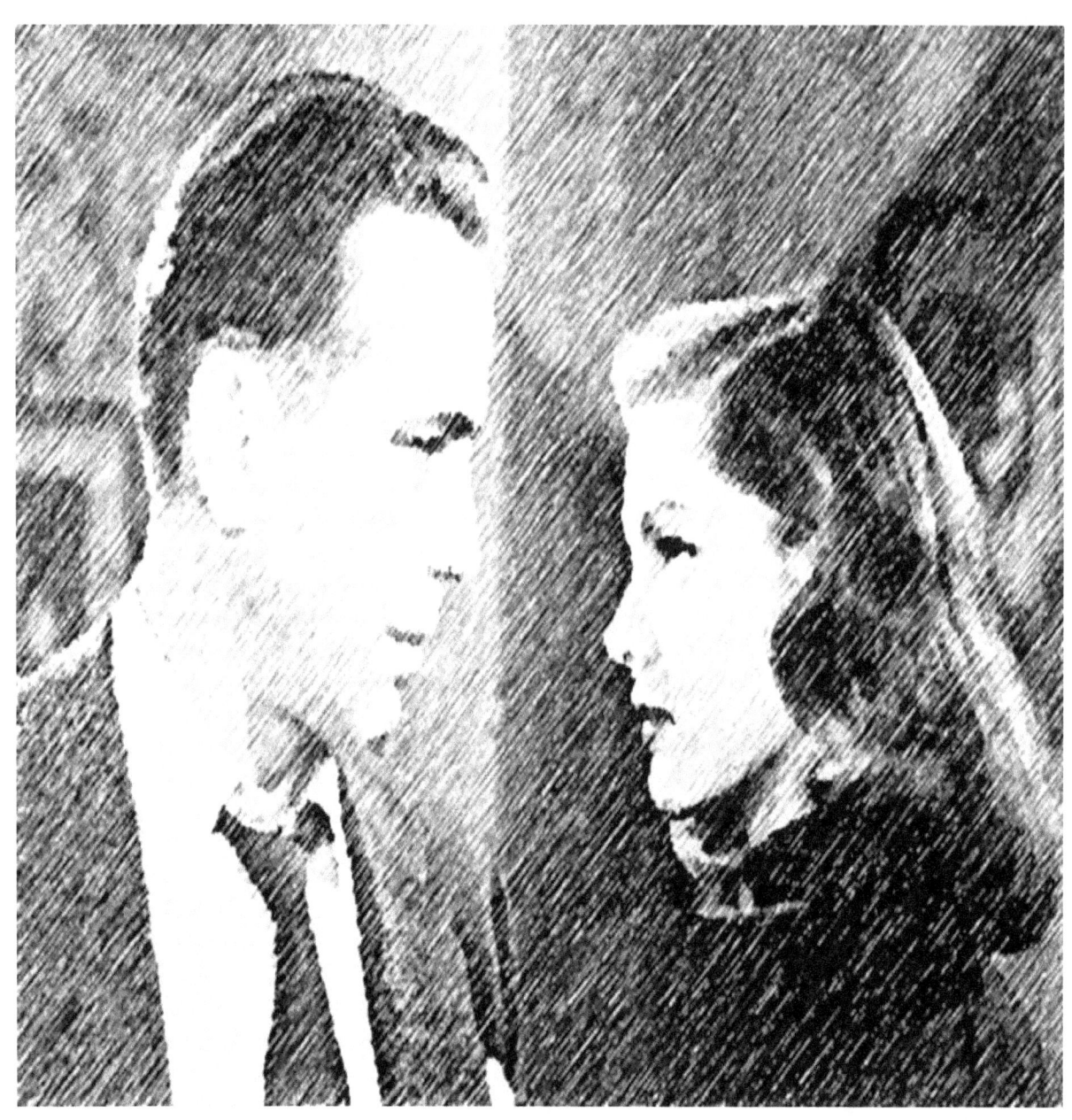

This page is intended for note taking

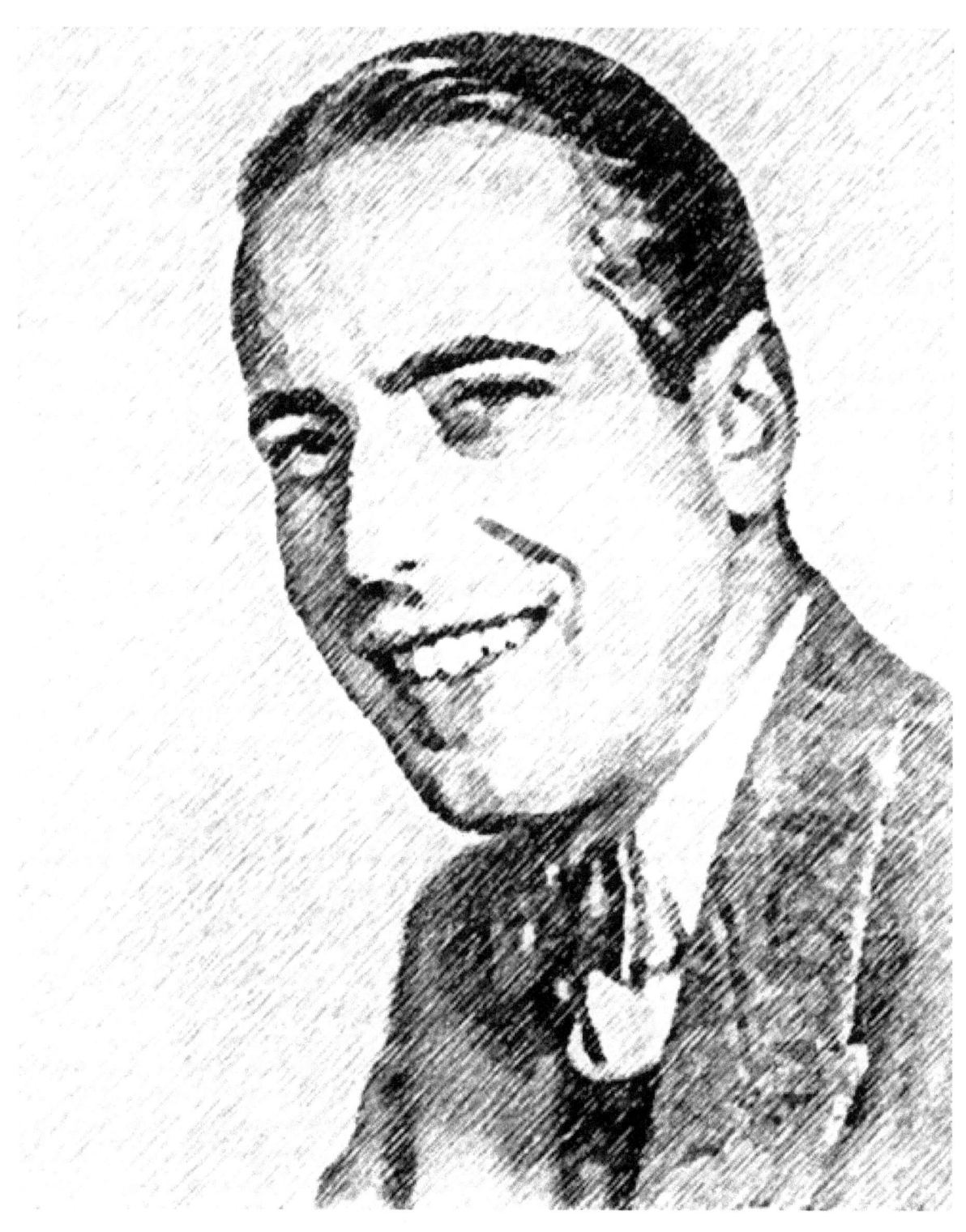

MEDICATION REMINDER

AM 1 X Daily	PM 2 X Daily	SUPPLEMENTS	NOTES

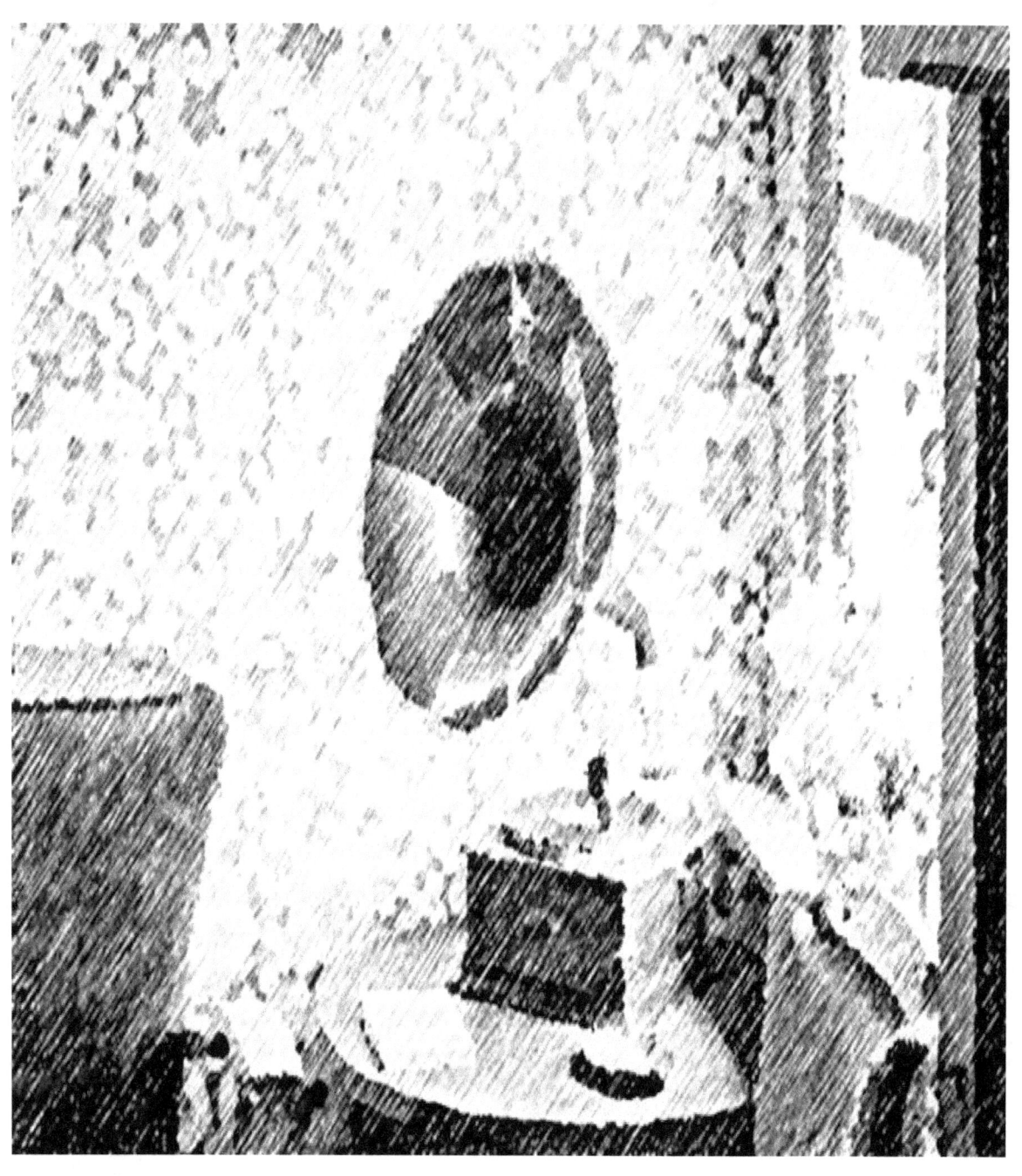

This page is intended for note taking

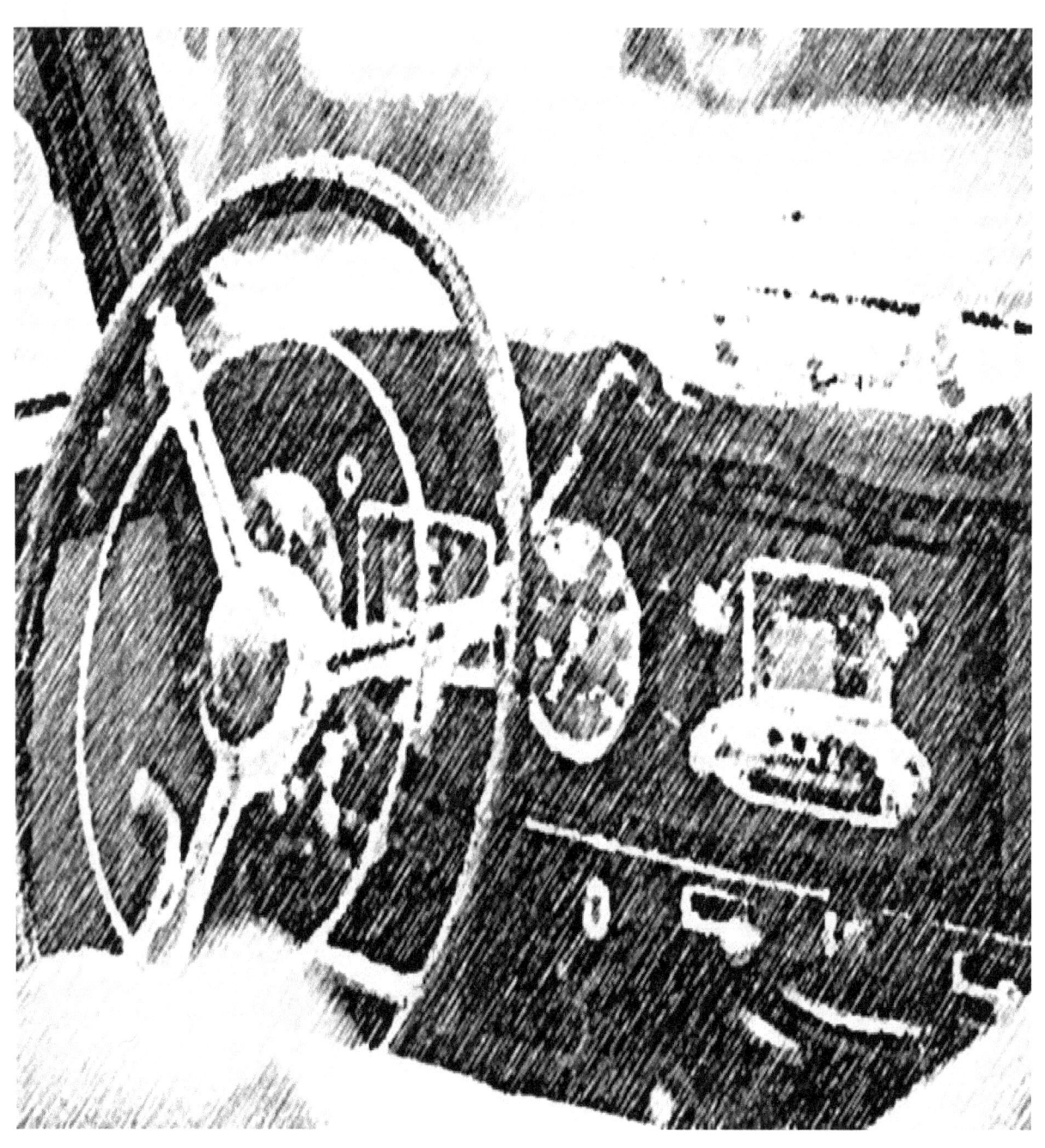

MEDICATION REMINDER

AM 1 X Daily	PM 2 X Daily	SUPPLEMENTS	NOTES

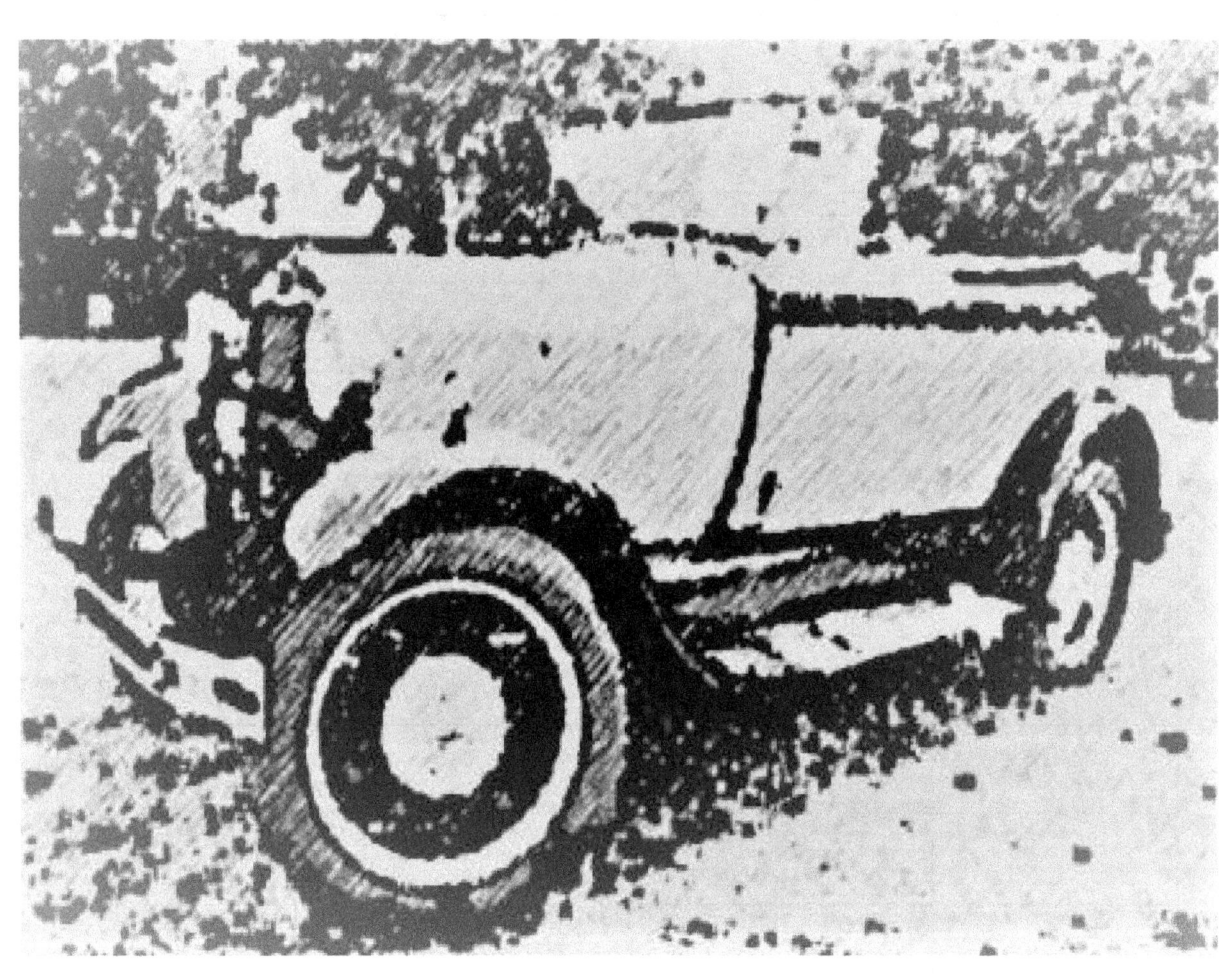

This page is intended for note taking

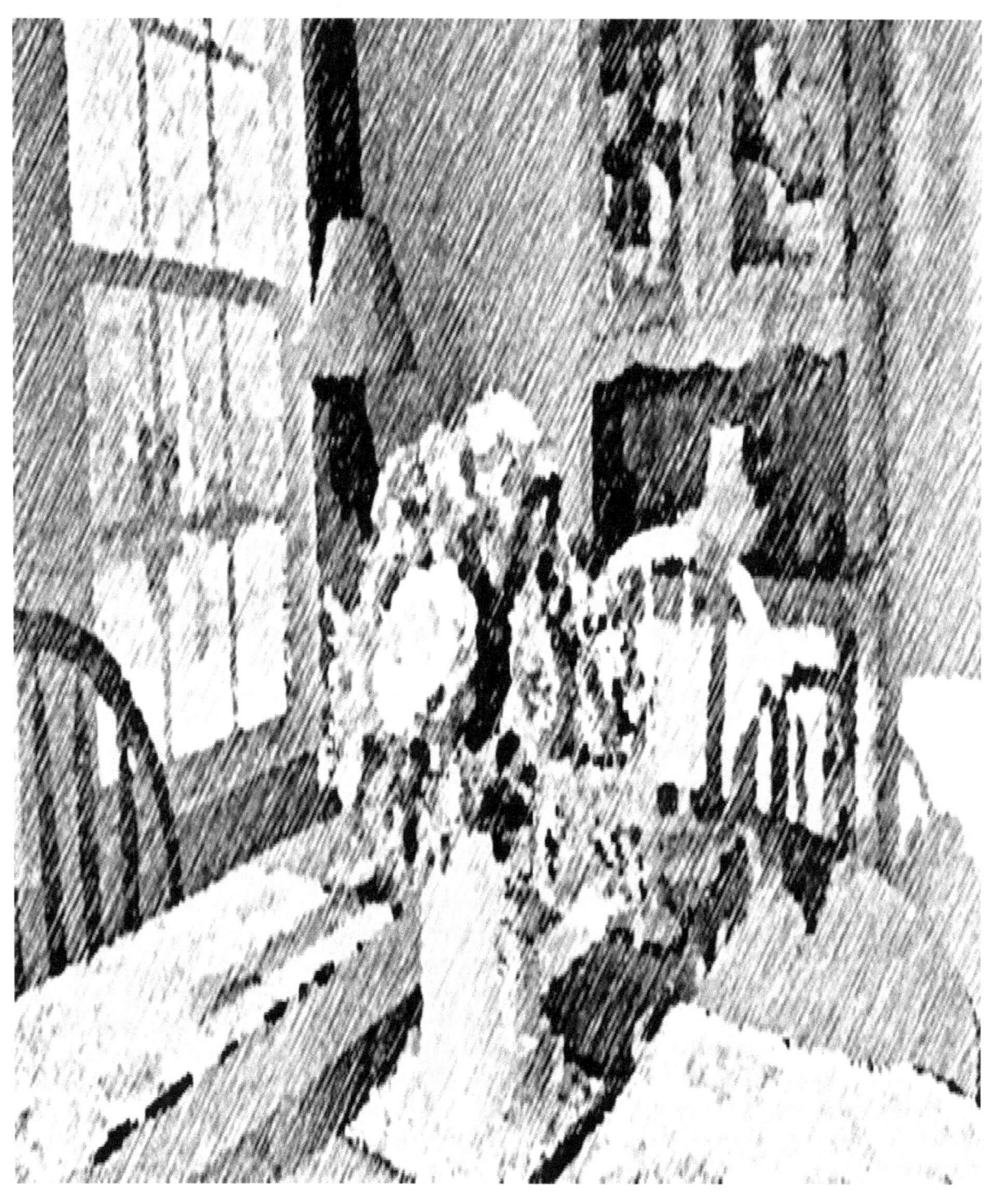

MEDICATION REMINDER

AM 1 X Daily	PM 2 X Daily	SUPPLEMENTS	NOTES

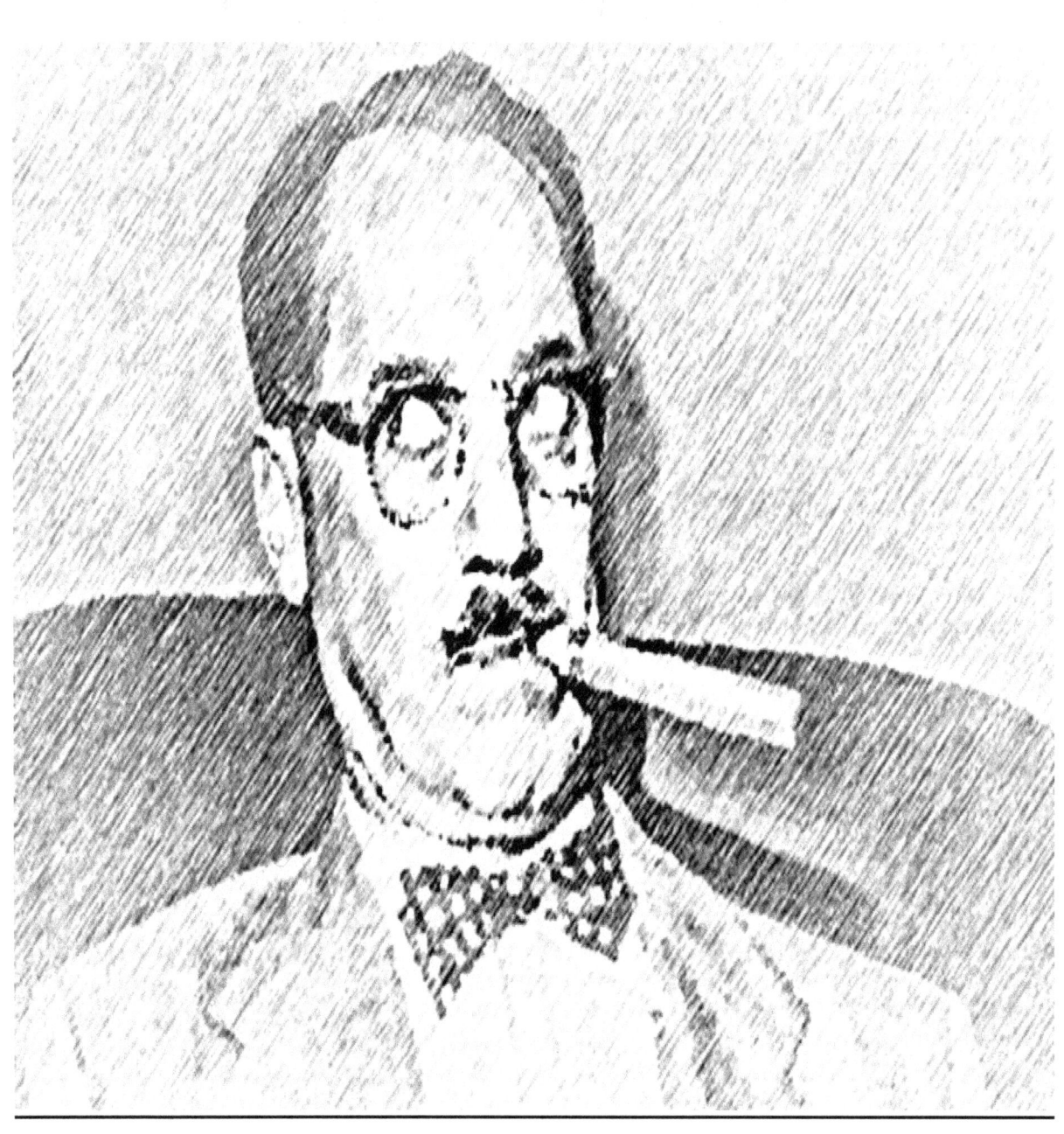

This page is intended for note taking

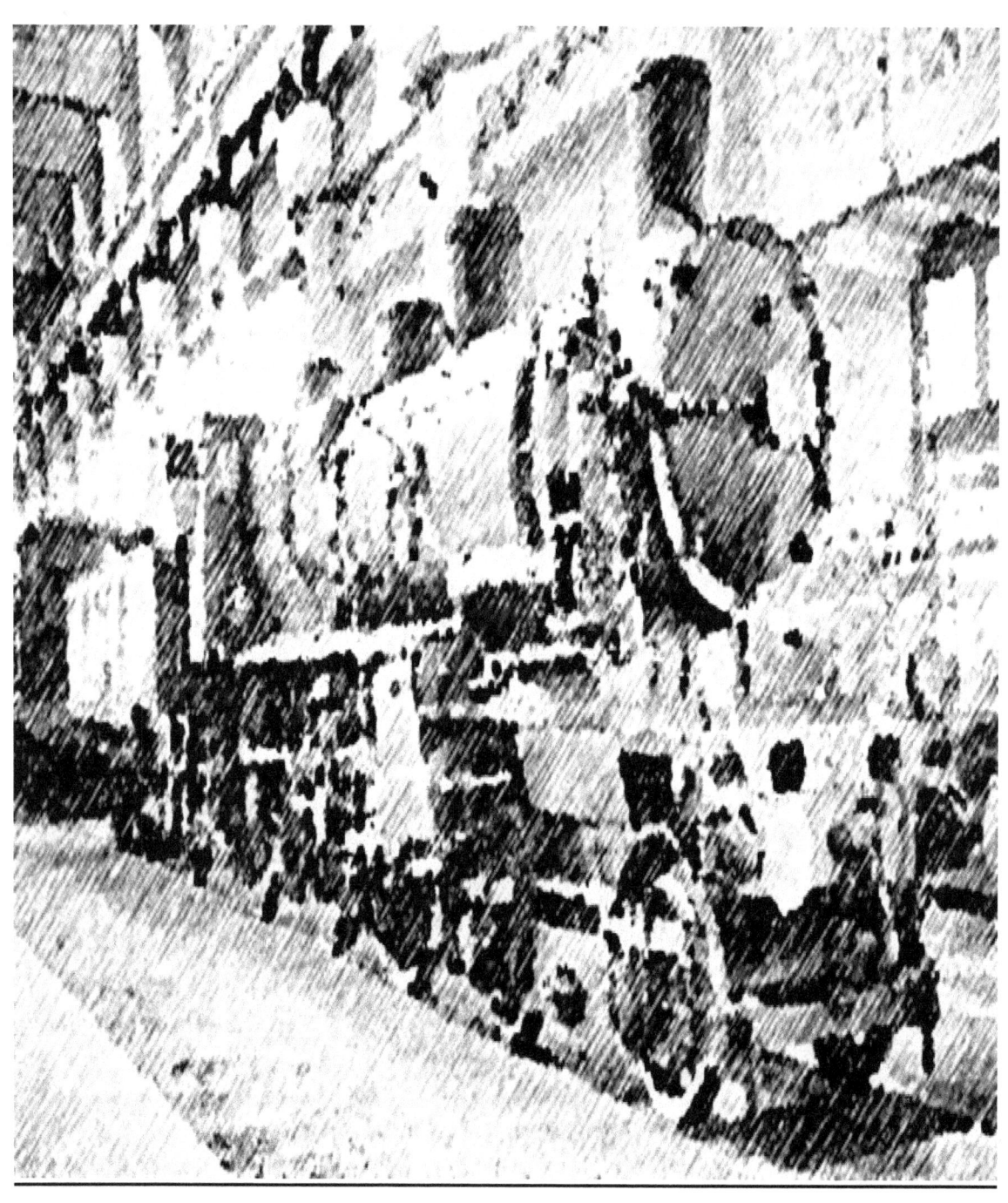

MEDICATION REMINDER

AM 1 X Daily	PM 2 X Daily	SUPPLEMENTS	NOTES

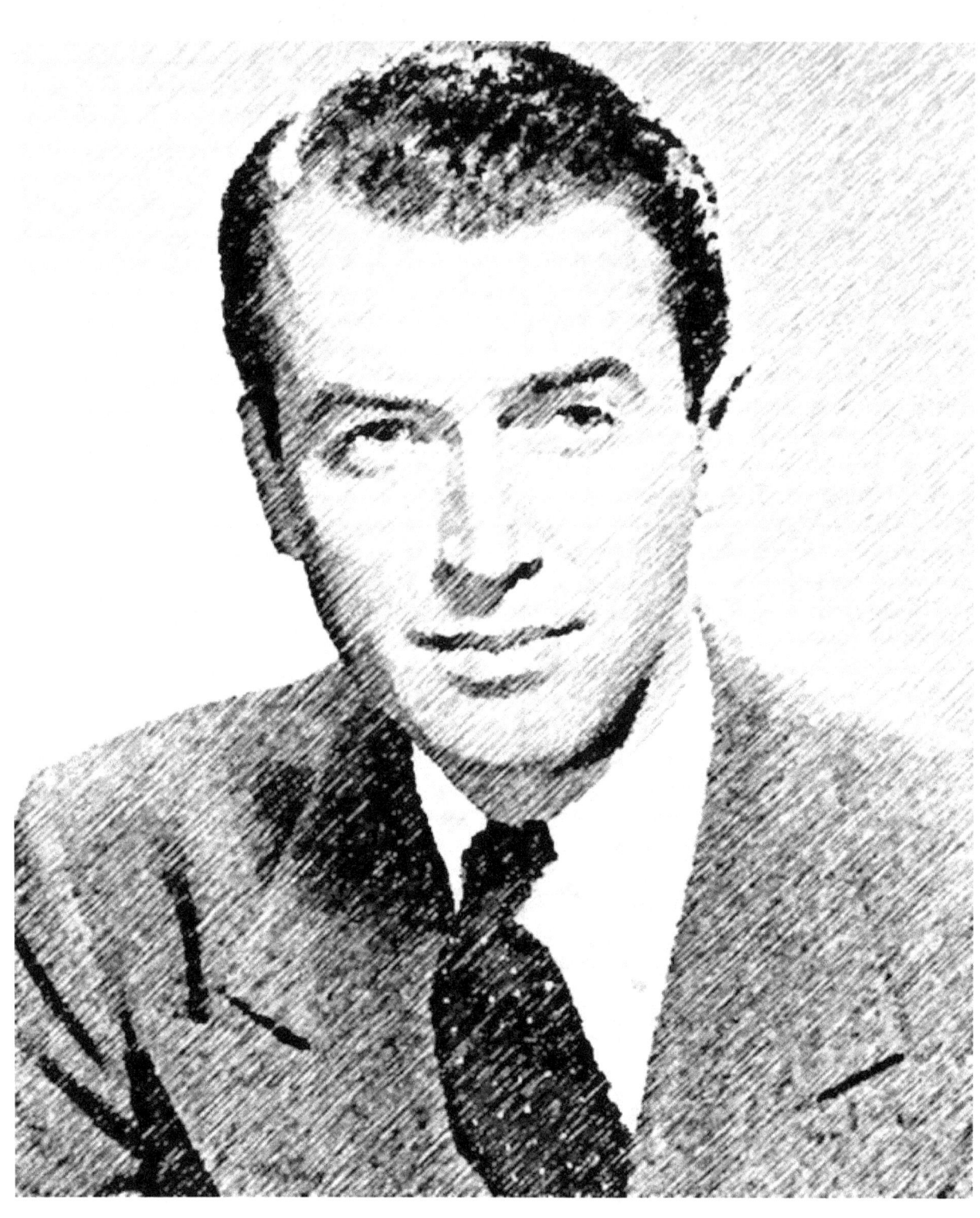

This page is intended for note taking

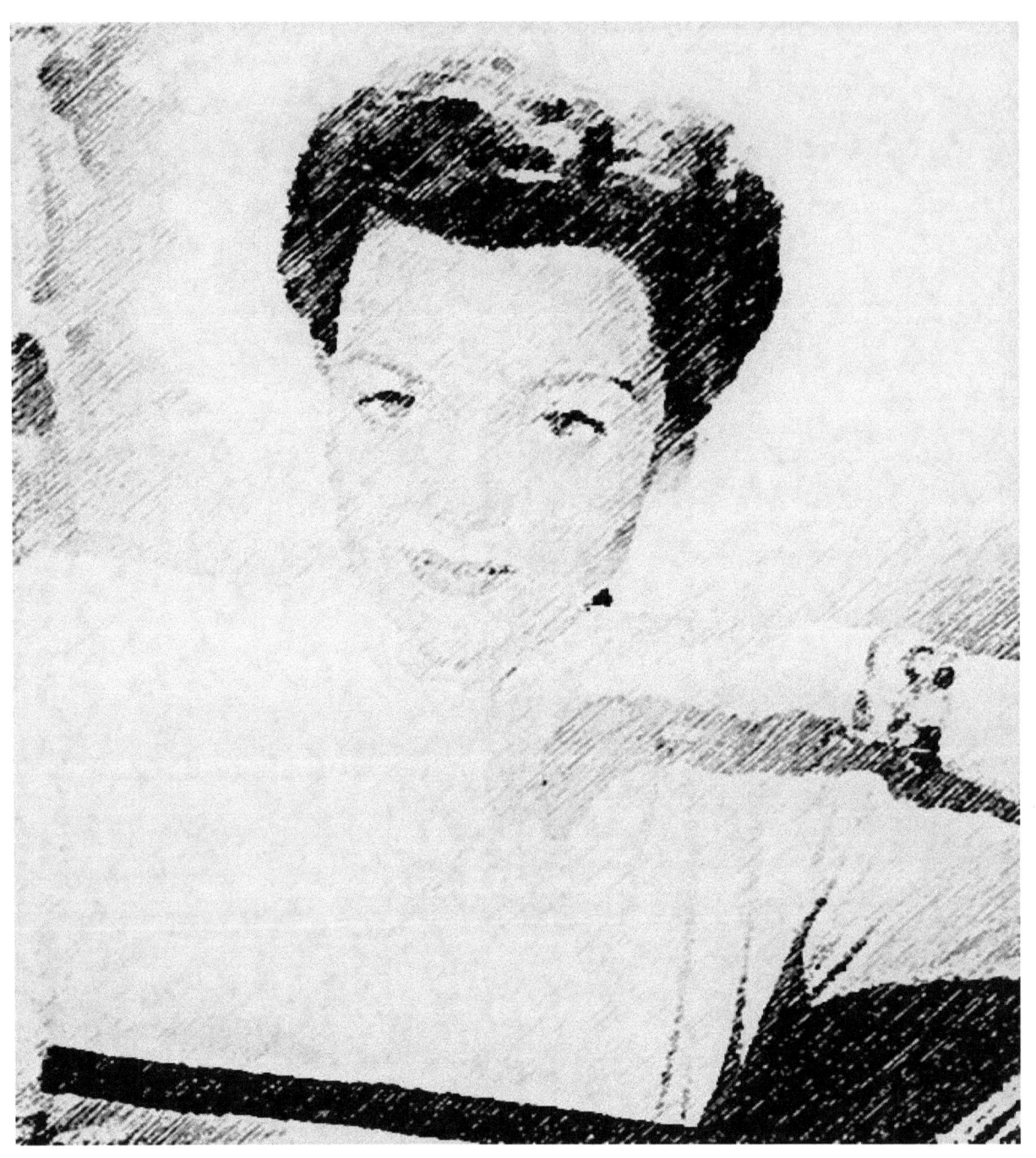

MEDICATION REMINDER

AM 1 X Daily	PM 2 X Daily	SUPPLEMENTS	NOTES

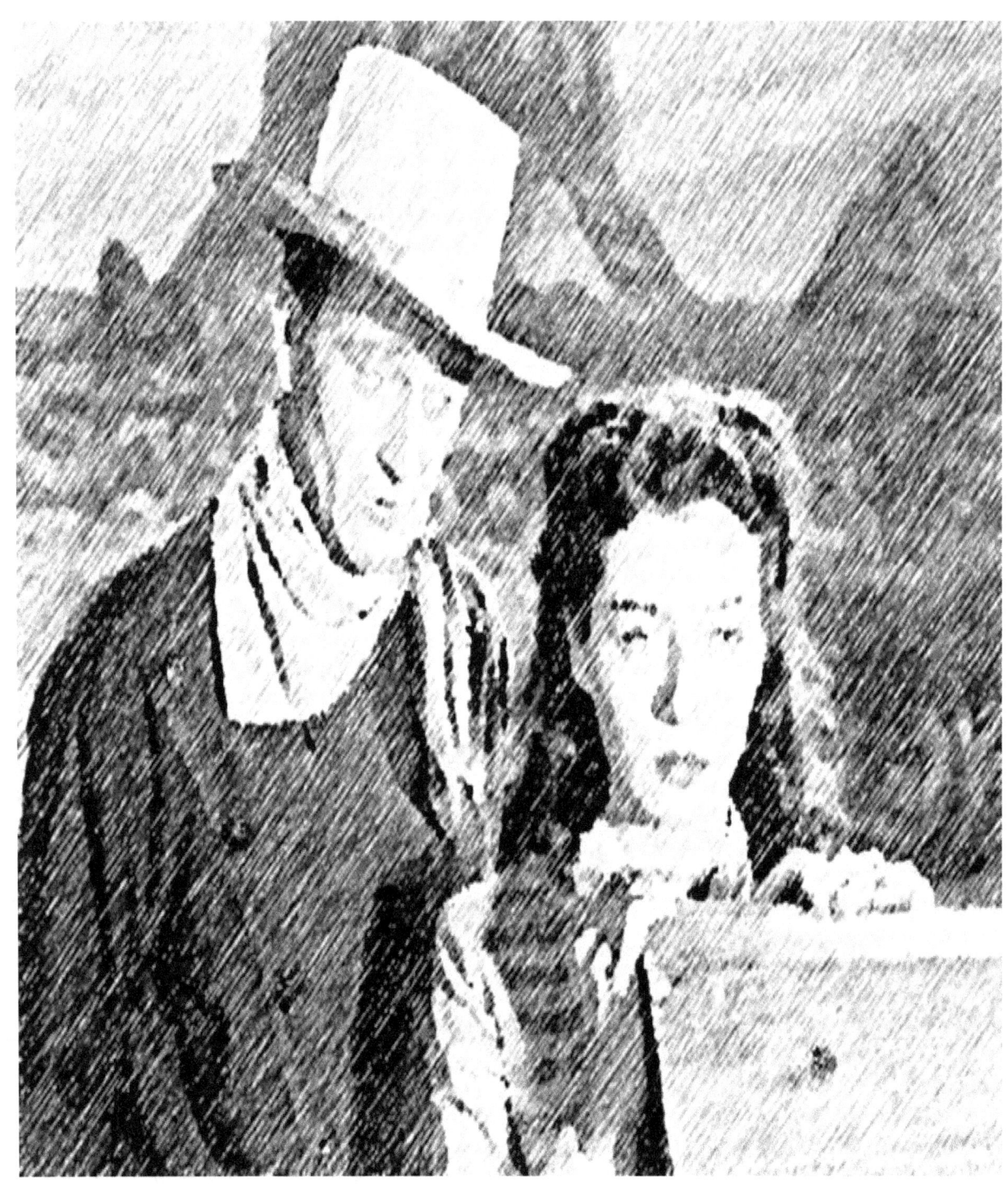

This page is intended for note taking

My Riddle Page

What did the honey bee say to the person that tried to take down his nest?

What did the cereal say to the milk, before being eaten?

What did the Christmas card say to the magazines, when placed it in the mailbox?

Answers Below:

Buzz Off - Cheerio - Greetings

MEDICATION REMINDER

AM 1 X Daily	PM 2 X Daily	SUPPLEMENTS	NOTES

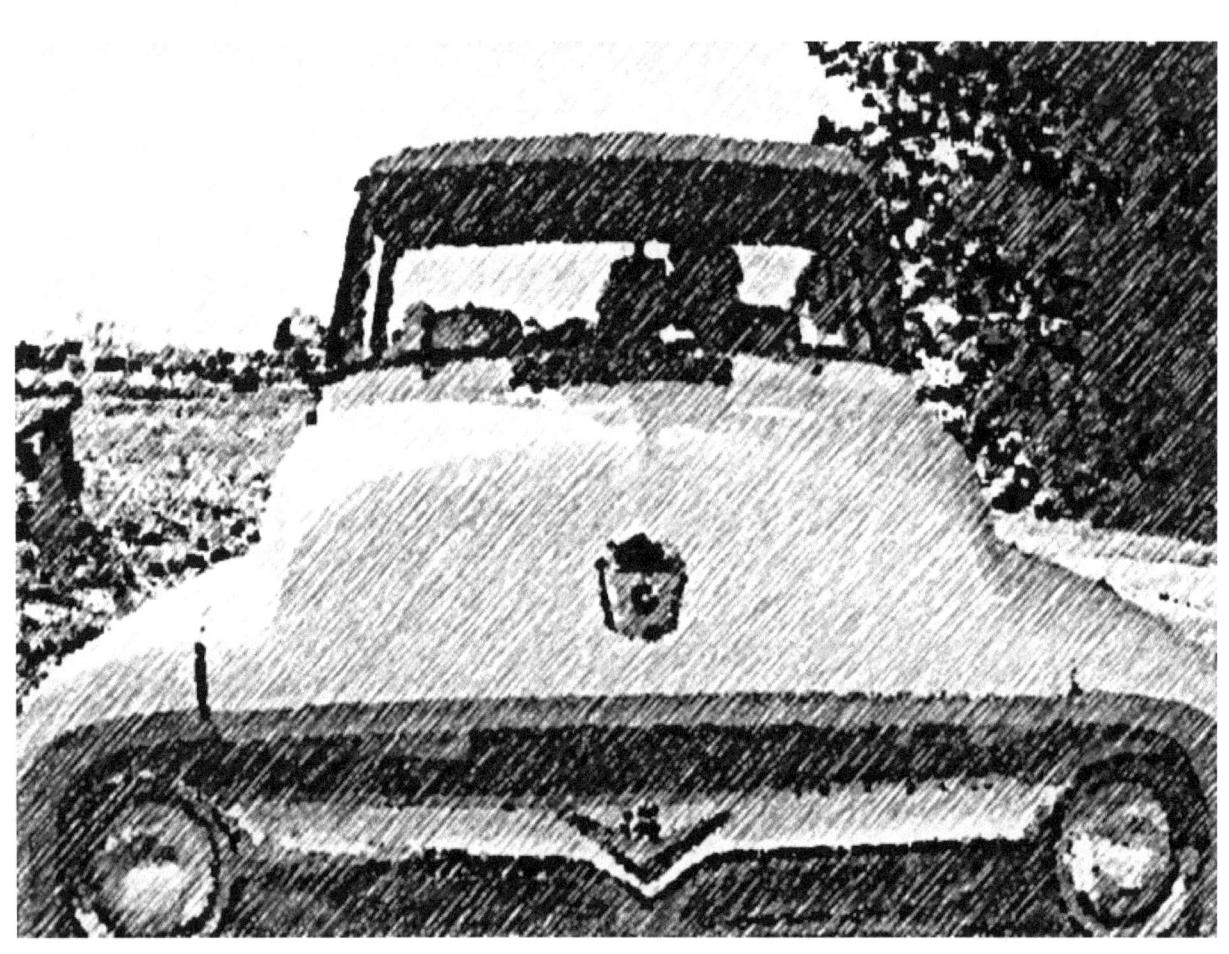

This page is intended for note taking

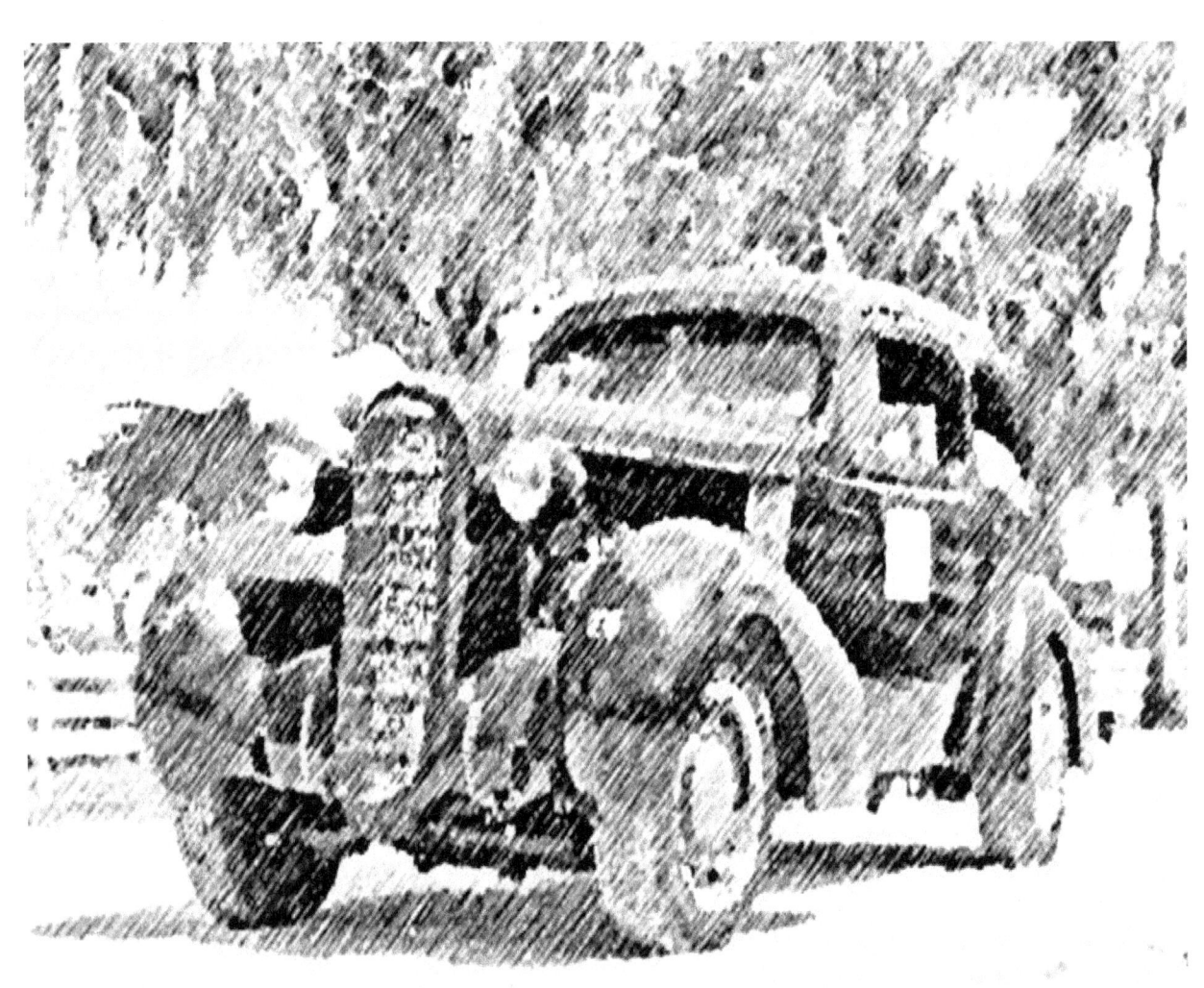

MEDICATION REMINDER

AM 1 X Daily	PM 2 X Daily	SUPPLEMENTS	NOTES

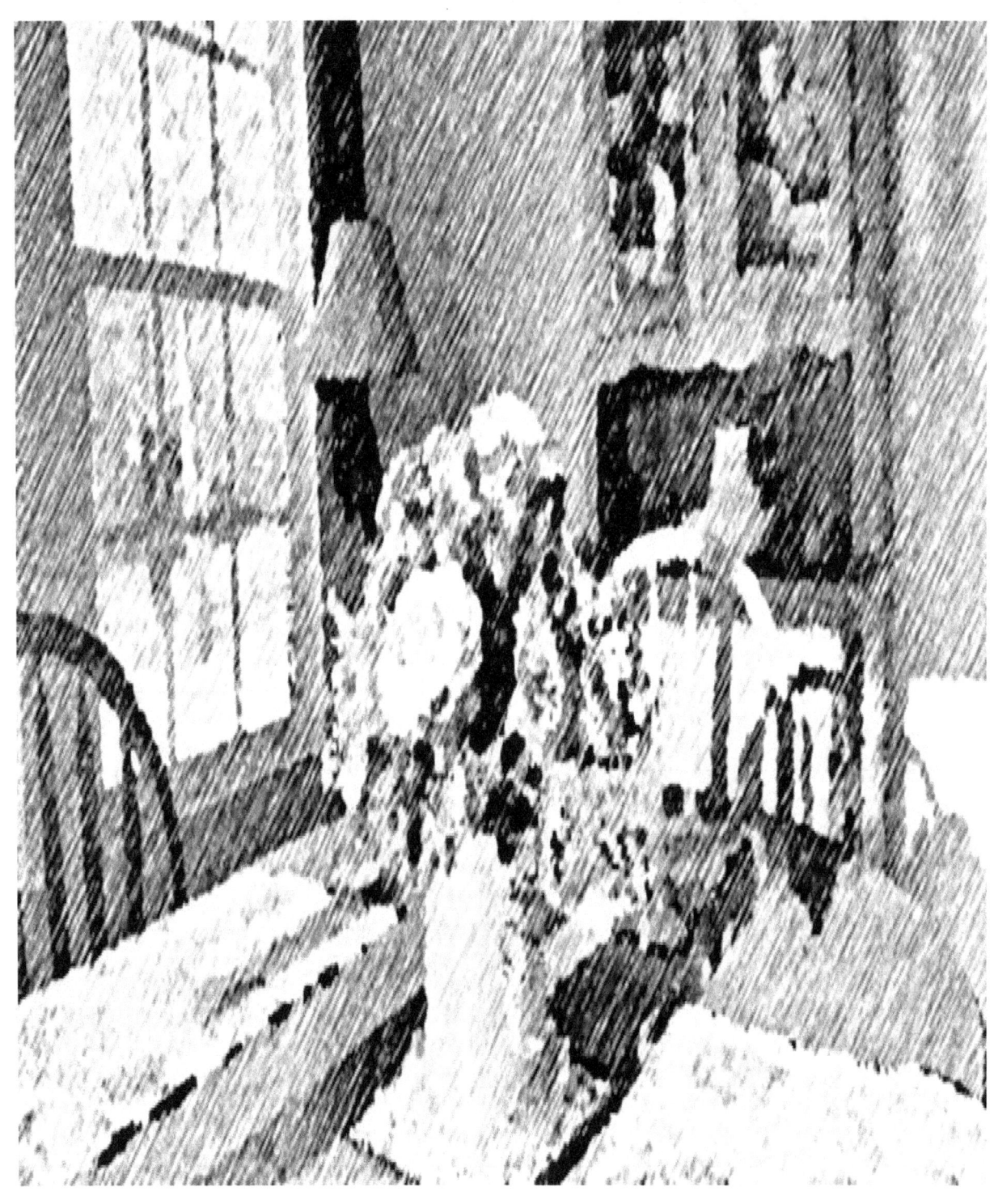

This page is intended for note taking

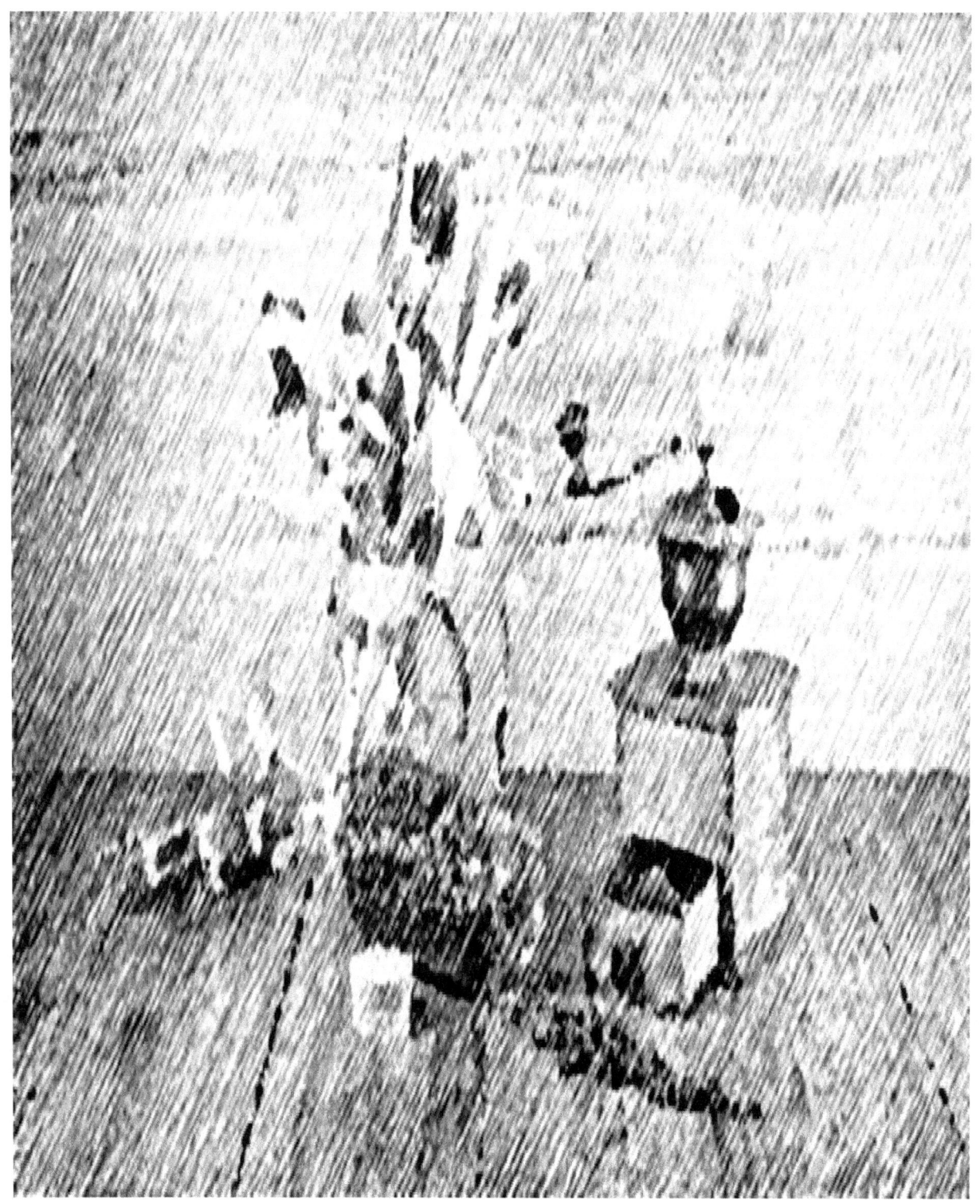

MEDICATION REMINDER

AM 1 X Daily	PM 2 X Daily	SUPPLEMENTS	Notes

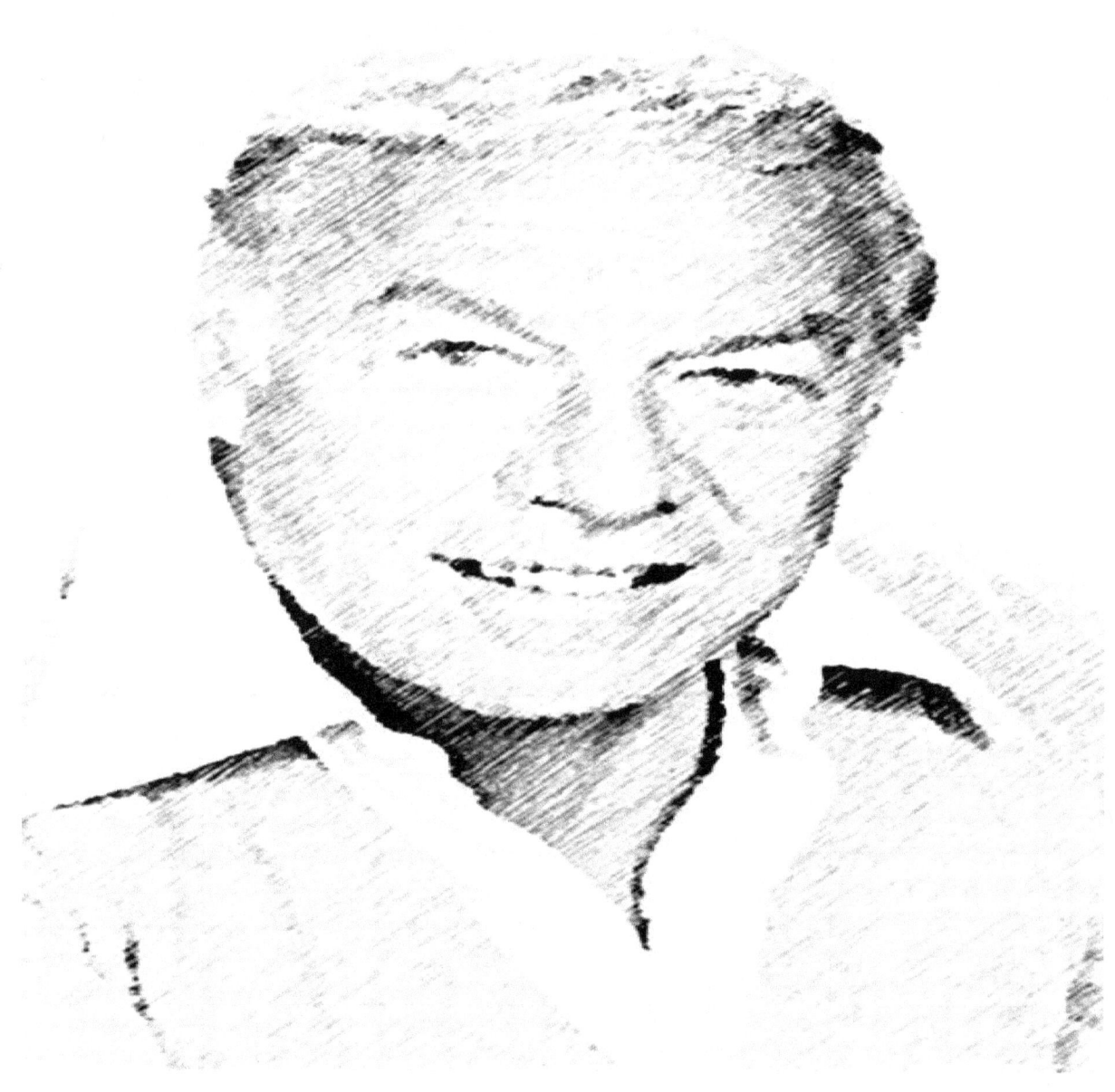

This page is intended for note taking

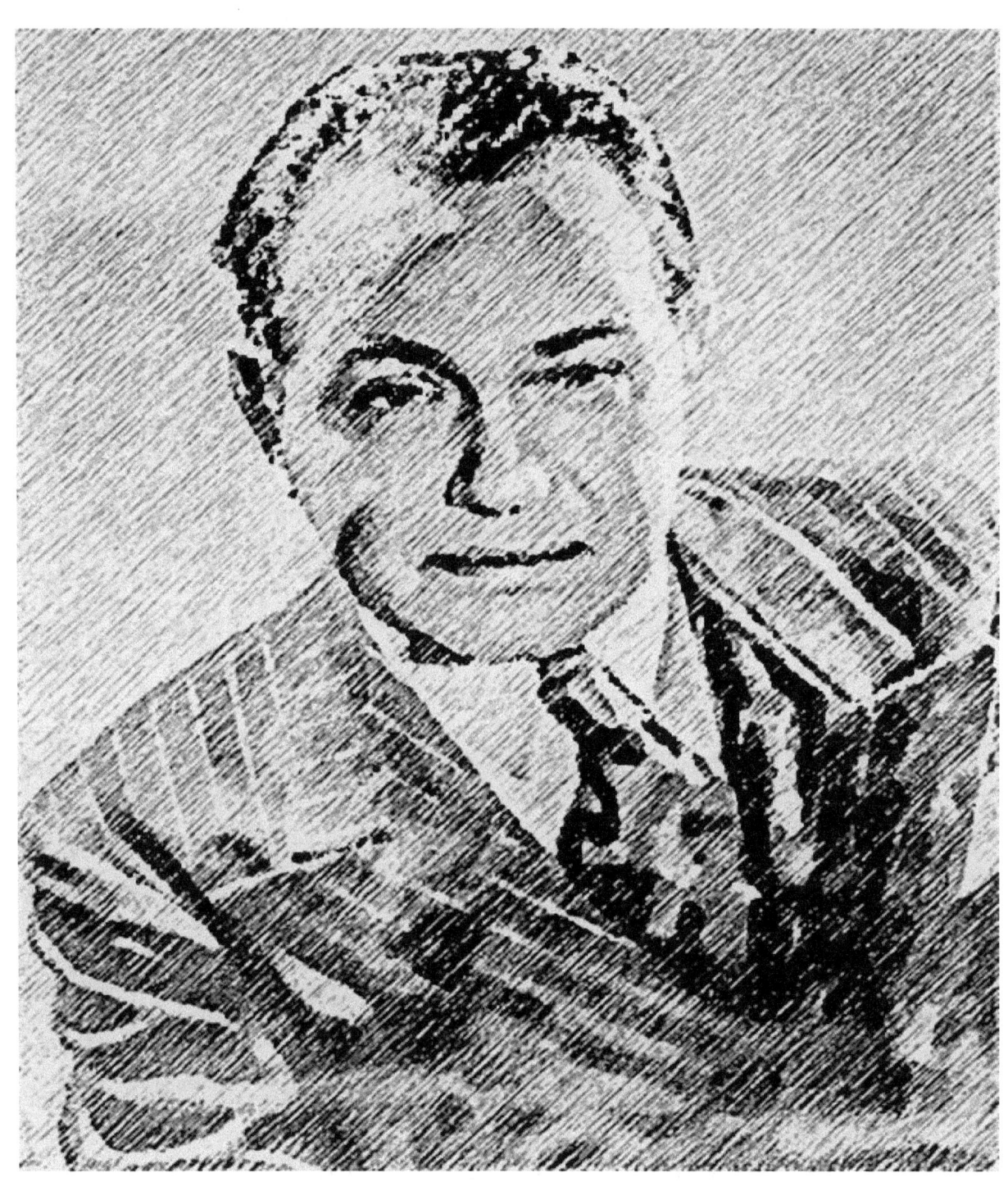

MEDICATION REMINDER

AM 1 X Daily	PM 2 X Daily	SUPPLEMENTS	NOTES

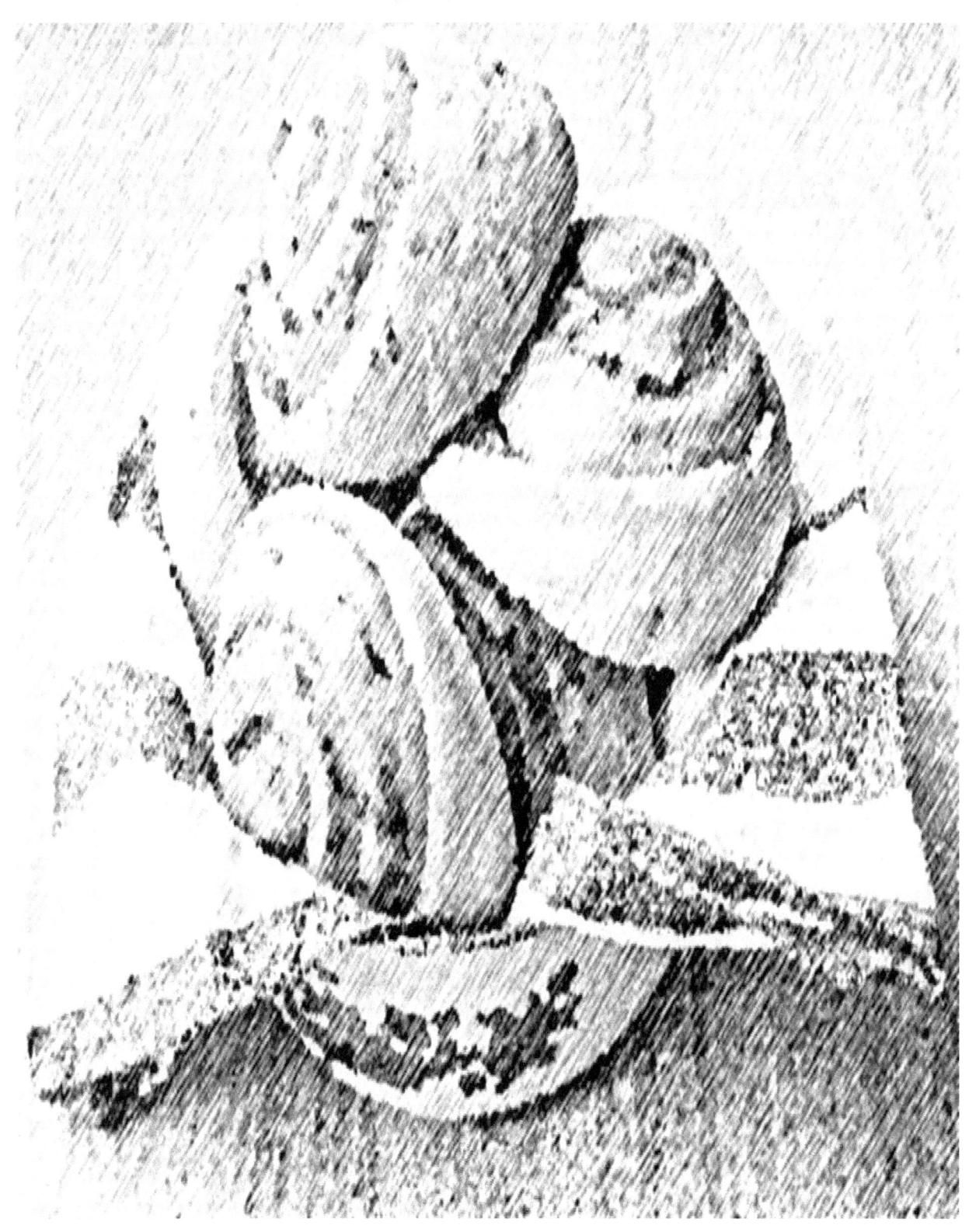

This page is intended for note taking

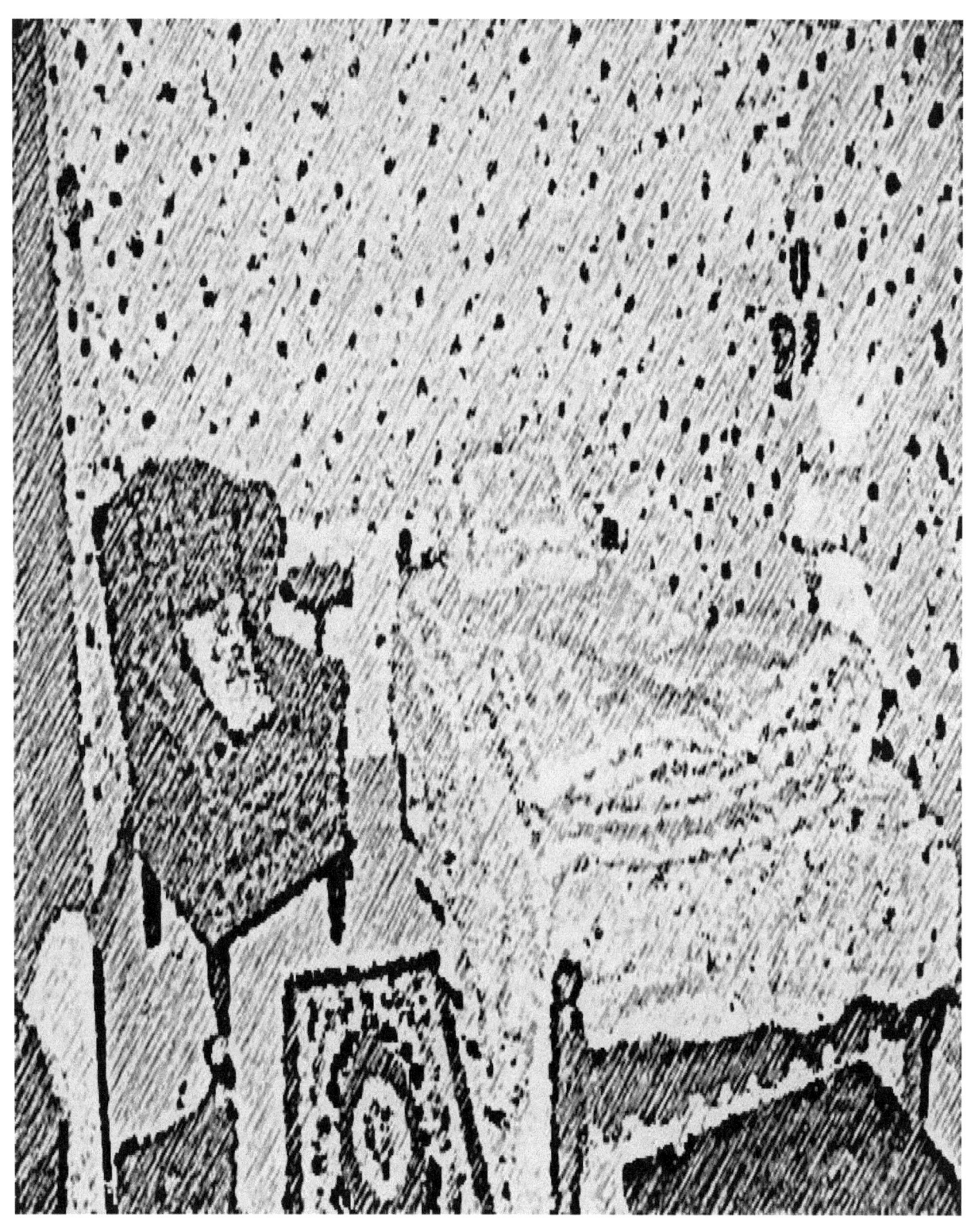

MEDICATION REMINDER

AM 1 X Daily	PM 2 X Daily	SUPPLEMENTS	NOTES

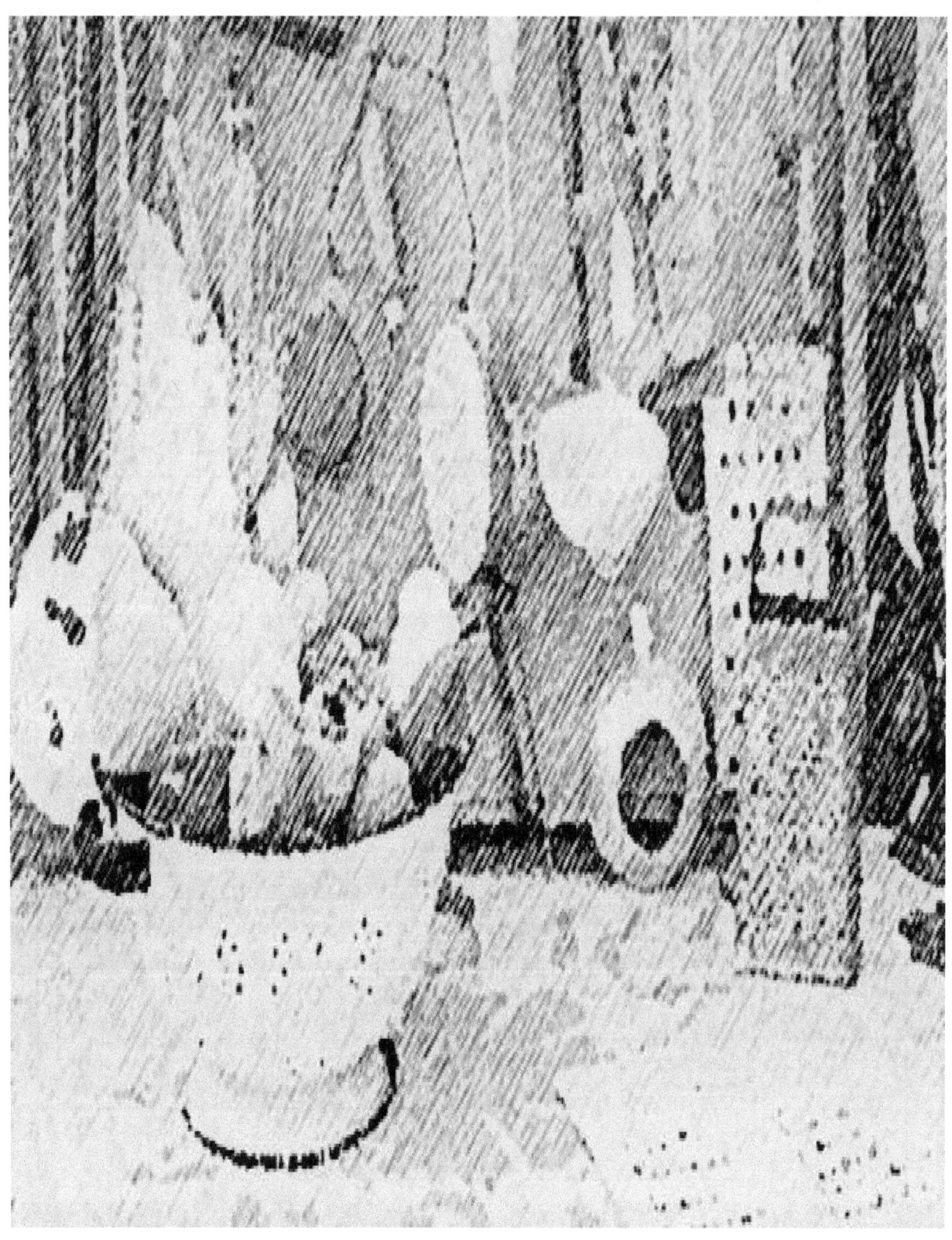

This page is intended for note taking

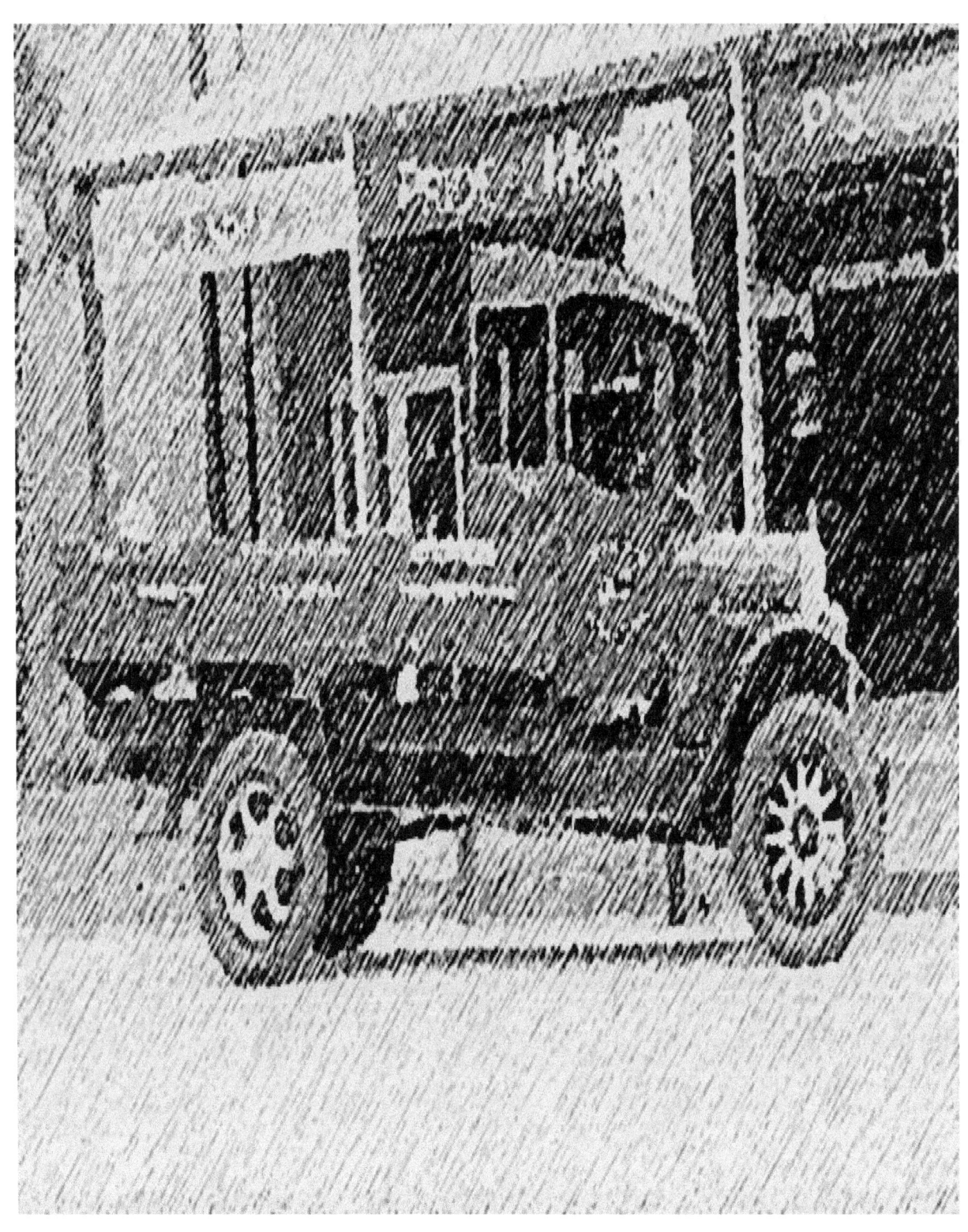

Senior Safety

1. Avoid falls by placing a mat in tub, while bathing and showering.

2. Wet spots on floors, must be wiped thoroughly.

3. Medical alert devices, should be considered for purchase if memory lose or balance are an issue.

4. When sitting for long periods of time, do some walking for at least 15 – 20 minutes daily.

5. Always avoid the use of steps if balance presents a problem.

Senior Safety

(continued)

6. Make sure to eat three balanced meals daily. Take stock in hot and cold cereals, meat, fresh fruits and dairy.

7. Drink at least 6 – 8 glasses of water daily to avoid dehydration.

8. Never use a stove top or oven to warm your home.

9. Have reliable family members ensure all heating and cooling systems are in place.

10. Always carry a phone whenever you leave a room. Dial 911 in case of any emergency.

MEDICATION REMINDER

AM 1X Daily	PM 2 X Daily	SUPPLEMENTS	NOTES

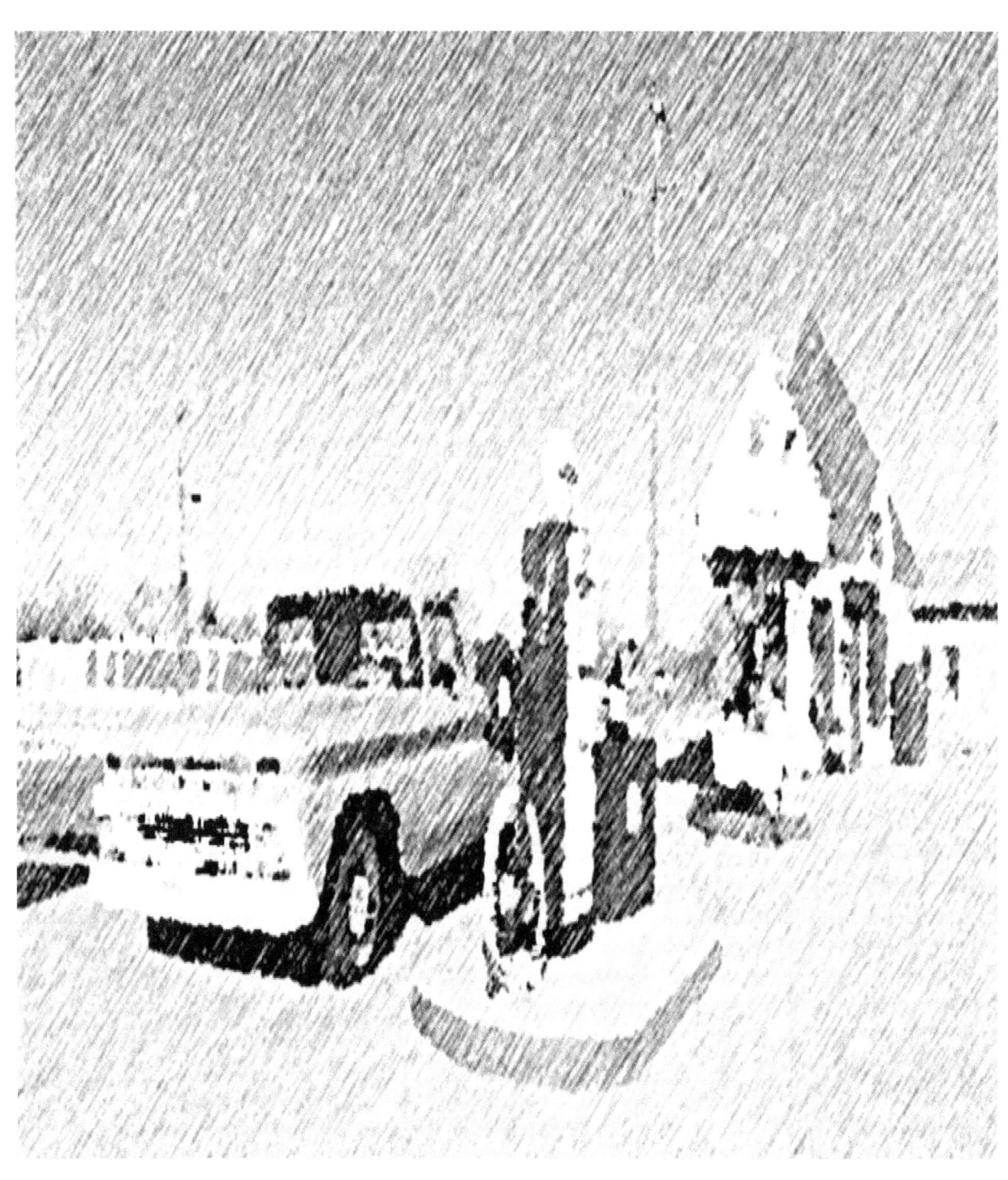

MEMORY GAME

(CIRCLE THE ANSWER BELOW)

Best choice for dinner	🍩 ☕ 🍝
Which day is coldest	☀️ ❄️ ⛅
Form of transportation	🛒 🪐 🚌
Tools for an artist	🎨 🔧🖌️ 🖌️
Carts groceries in store	🛒 🚗 🧺
For health and hygiene	🚿 🪮 🧴

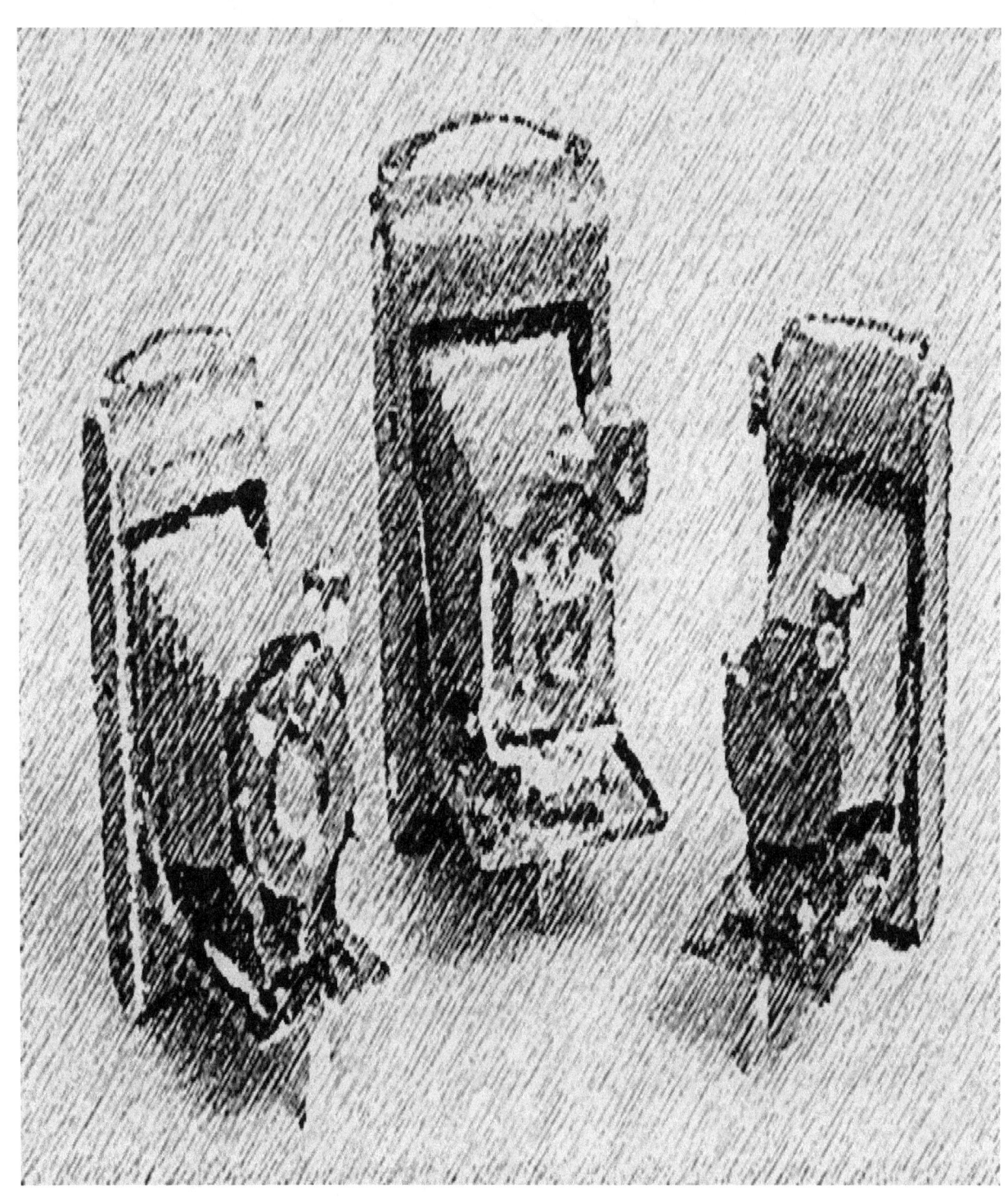

This page is intended for note taking

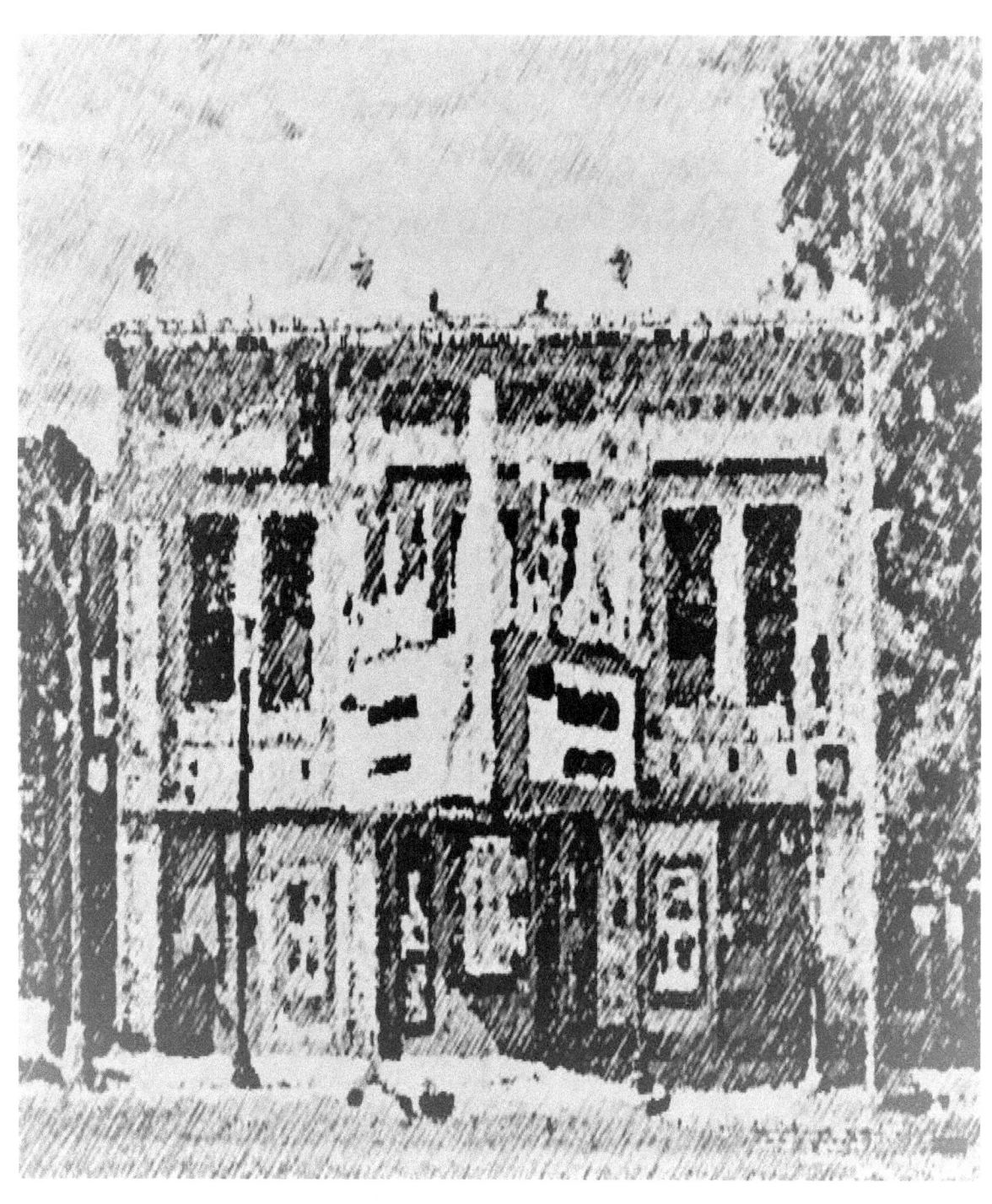

MEDICATION REMINDER

AM 1 X Daily	PM 2 X Daily	SUPPLEMENTS	NOTES

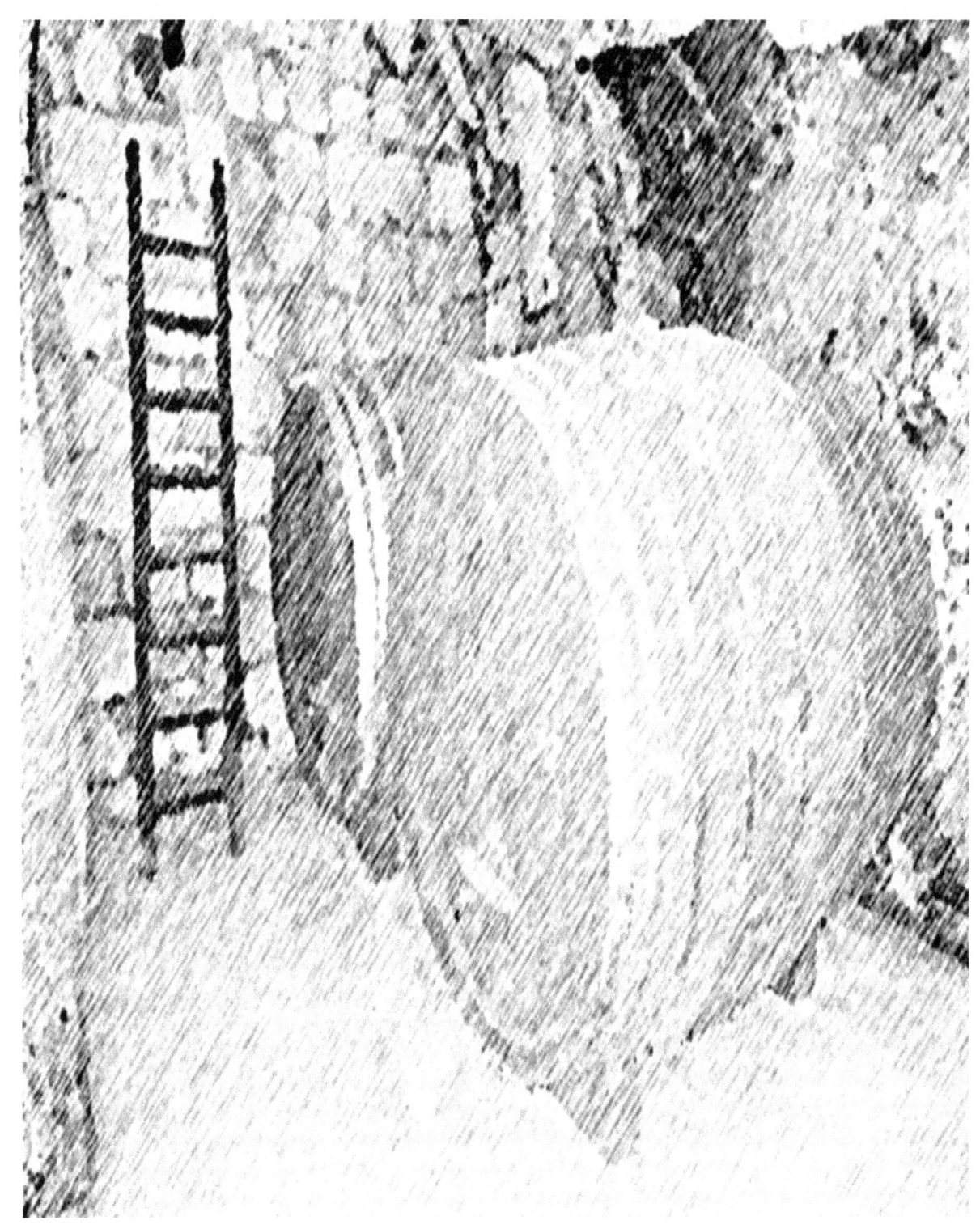

This page is intended for note taking

TIME

THOUGH TIME CONTINUES TO
PASS US BY

WE'LL ALWAYS REMAIN AHEAD

THE TRACKS WE LAID BEHIND

WILL OPEN UP NEW ONES AHEAD

By: Mary L. Boccadoro

MEDICATION REMINDER

AM 1 X Daily	PM 2 X Daily	SUPPLEMENTS	NOTES

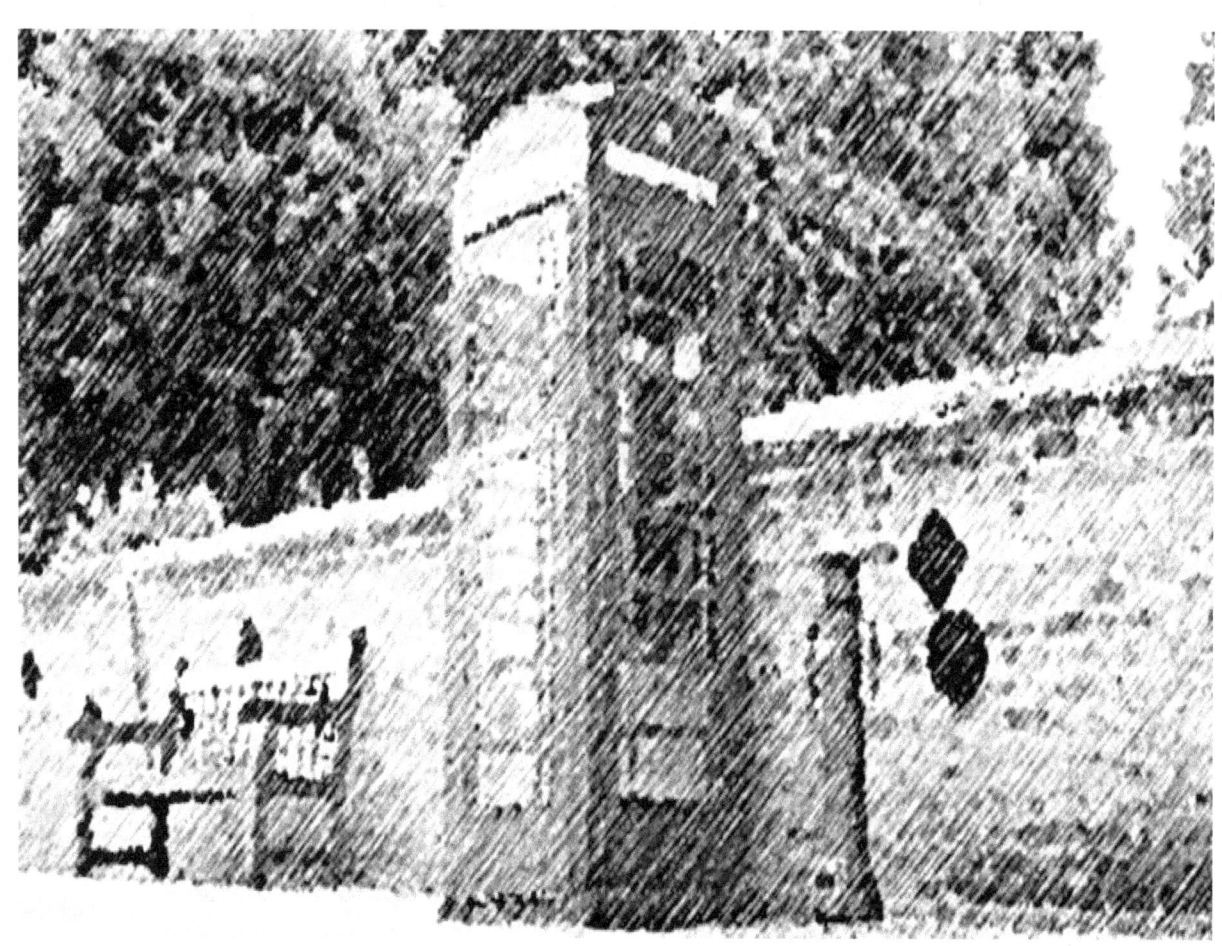

This page is intended for note taking

CIRCLE 8 MUST DO'S DAILY

TAKE CARE OF PERSONAL FINANCES	TAKE A STROLL ALONG THE BEACH
DO SOME KNITTING	TAKE MEDICATIONS ON MY OWN
GROW A VEGTABLE GARDEN	GO ON A CRRUISE
VISIT A MUSEUM	DO ALL TYPES OF SHOPPING MYSELF
CLEAN MY HOUSE	SING IN AN OPERA
DRIVE OR FIND MY OWN TRANSPORTATION	WASH MY CLOTHES
GO HIKING ON A NATURE TRAIL	GO SQUARE DANCING
LOOK UP TEEPHONE NUMBERS	MAKE AND PLAN MY MEALS

This page is intended for note taking

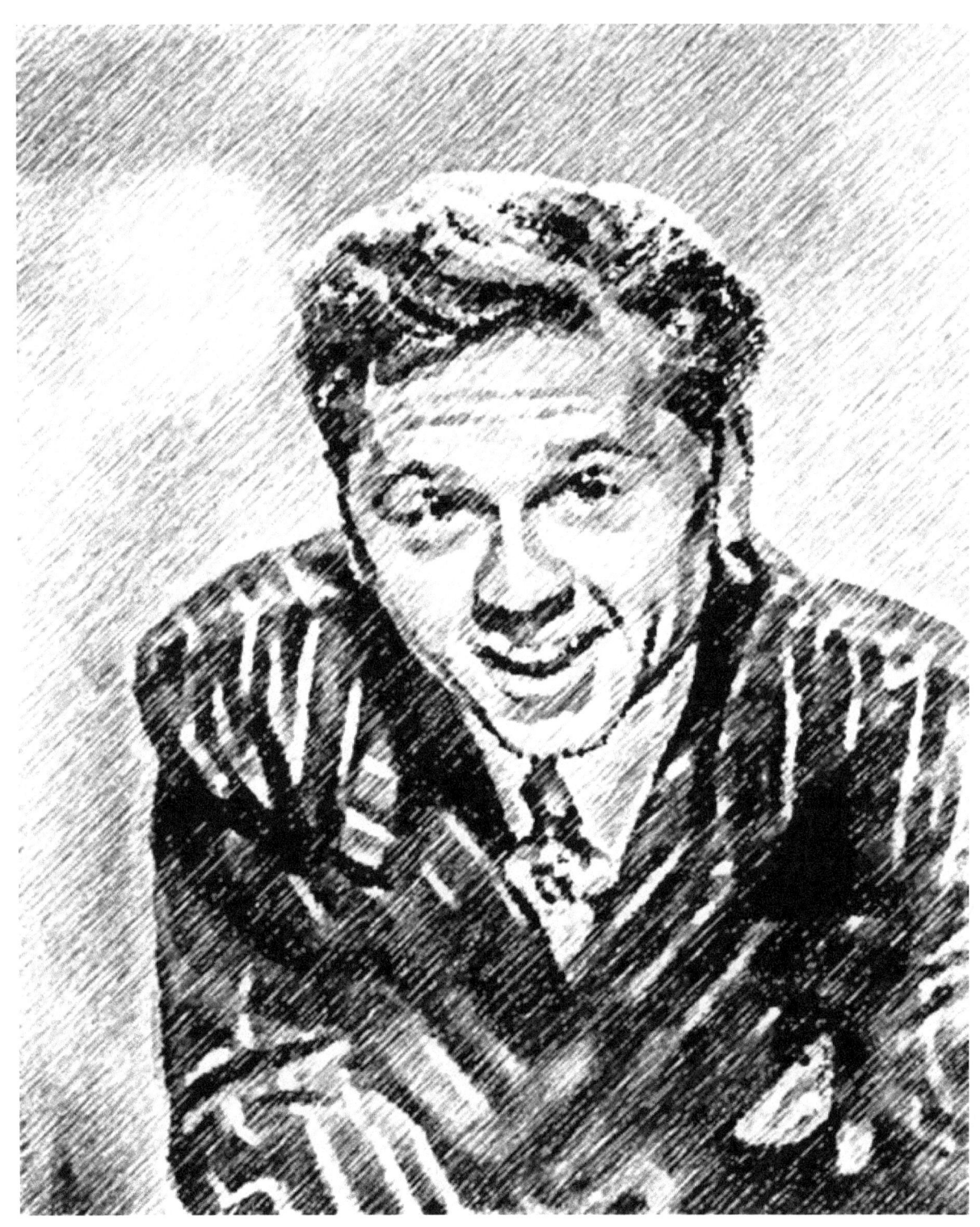

MEDICATION REMINDER

AM 1 X DAILY	PM 2 X DAIY	SUPPLEMENTS	NOTES

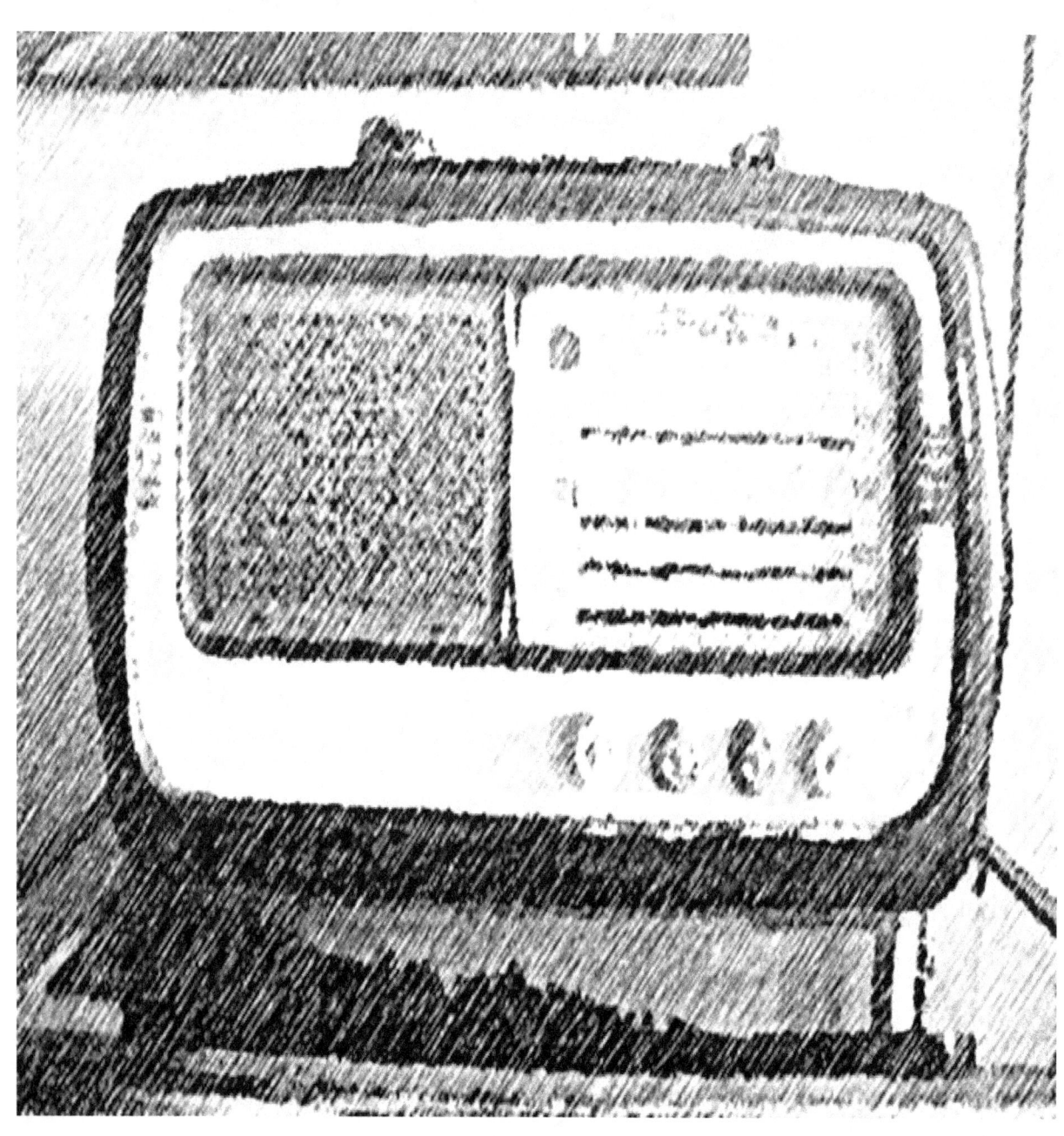

This page is intended for note taking

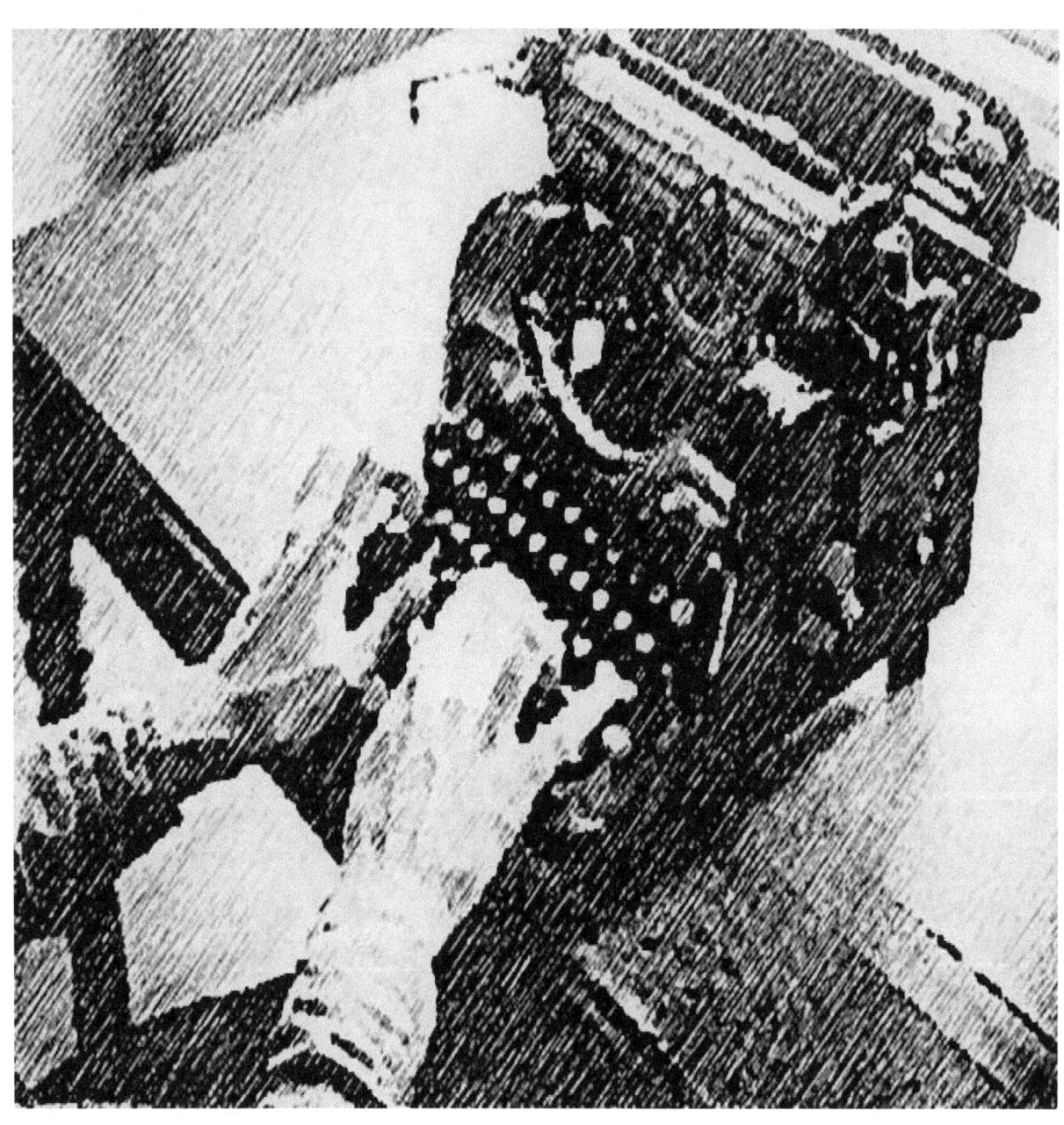

MEDICATION REMINDER

AM 1 X DAILY	PM 2 X DAIY	SUPPLEMENTS	NOTES

My Riddle Page:

1. **What did the angry janitor say to the floor while putting away his mop?**

2. **What did the broken finger say to the hand?**

3. **What did the peanut butter say to the empty jar?**

4. Answers: You're all washed up - thumb's up – Oh nuts

Name	Address	Phone

FOR MORE INFORMATION:
(CHECK OUT THE URL'S BELOW)

MY AMAZON AUTHOR PAGE:
(BIO AND BOOK RELEASES)

https://www.Amazon.com/e/BO1AEF7MVU

OR

VISIT MY FACEBOOK PAGE:

https://tinyurl.com/y79ggtac

(FOR SAMPLES OF MY WORK)

https://tinyurl.com/2atogy

Name	Address	Phone

www.ingramcontent.com/pod-product-compliance
Lightning Source LLC
Chambersburg PA
CBHW062216220526
45471CB00009B/3219